D1135234

COUNTY AND VOLUNTARY SCHOOLS

# County and Voluntary Schools

FOURTH EDITION

by

## SIR WILLIAM ALEXANDER

*Secretary, Association of Education Committees*

and

## F. BARRACLOUGH, C.B.E., M.A.

*Formerly Honorary Treasurer, Association of Education Committees*

## ERRATA

1. **Page 34.** Note (*h*), at the end of the 3rd paragraph:
For the words: 'So order, as he has power to do',
*Read:* 'order, as he has power to do, that neither
relief is available,'

2. **Page 79.** Note (*i*) does not refer to the words 'other
buildings' in the text, but to the words 'for the other
half' in Note (*e*).

COUNCILS & EDUCATION PRESS LTD
10 Queen Anne Street, London W1
1967

FOURTH EDITION 1967

*Set in The Times New Roman Series*

*Made and printed in Great Britain by*
STAPLES PRINTERS LIMITED, LONDON AND ST ALBANS

# Contents

# PREFACE TO THE FOURTH EDITION

The third edition of *County and Voluntary Schools* was published four years ago. Yet, mainly, though not entirely, because of a number of new enactments since then, it has been necessary to make substantial changes in the text and notes for this fourth edition. The principal revisions have been dictated by the Education Act, 1967, which goes right beyond the settlement of 1944. Between 1944 and 1959, amending Acts gave additional financial assistance to the managers and governors of many aided and special agreement schools, and some restrictions were removed from managers and governors of controlled schools. Nevertheless, the general principles of the 1944 settlement were retained, with the result that some new aided schools were built without any exchequer aid, and others with only a fraction of such aid. In addition, some controlled schools had to give place to county schools. Under the Education Act, 1967, the maximum level of the exchequer grant towards the capital expenditure on aided and special agreement schools is raised once again, this time from 75 to 80 per cent, with a corresponding increase in grant towards their external repair. But that is a minor change. The significant change made by the new Act for aided and special agreement schools is that exchequer aid at the rate of 80 per cent is to be given to all aided schools whose establishment or enlargement is approved, and to all special agreement schools whose enlargement is approved. Having regard to the considerable powers exercised by managers and governors of aided and special agreement schools, it was not surprising that the new provisions were described on the second reading of the Bill as a generous settlement that should remain on the statute book for a very long time. Matching concessions are made in the 1967 Act for controlled schools, which are primarily the concern of the Church of England. Above all, one object of the new Act is to enable all kinds of voluntary schools to play their full part in the reorganization of secondary schools on comprehensive lines. Some of the changes embodied in the Education Act, 1967, do not operate until April 1st, 1967, and this fourth edition of this book deals with the position from that date.

W. P. A.

F. B.

# I. INTRODUCTION

## 1. *Local Education Authority and Divisional Executive*

In a county borough, the county borough council are the local education authority (*a*); in a county, the county council. In Greater London, the council of an outer London borough are the local education authority, and in the remainder of Greater London (known as the Inner London Education Area) the Greater London Council, acting by means of a special committee, are the local education authority (*b*). Functions of the local education authority may be exercised on behalf of the council by the education committee (*c*). In most counties there are one or more divisional executives (*d*), exercising functions on behalf of the local education authority. Throughout this book, the term 'authority', or 'local education authority', is to be construed as the council, or their education committee, or divisional executive, according to the circumstances of the case.

### NOTES

(*a*) **Local Education Authority.** – See S.6 (1) of the Education Act, 1944.

(*b*) **Greater London.** – See S.30 of the London Government Act, 1963.

(*c*) **Education Committee.** – See S.6 (2) and §8 of Part II of the First Schedule of the Education Act, 1944. Under §10 of Part II of that schedule, a subcommittee of the Education Committee can exercise functions of the L.E.A.

(*d*) **Divisional Executives.** – See S.6 (3) and §2 of Part III of the First Schedule of the Education Act, 1944, as amended by the Education Act, 1946.

## 2. *Some Common Definitions*

Five important definitions of terms frequently used throughout the text in relation to county and voluntary schools, are given here, as follows:

**School Premises.** The school premises (*a*) consist of the site, the playing fields (whether detached or not from the site), and all the buildings on them, except the teacher's dwelling-house (*b*).

**Site.** The site (*c*) of a school does not include the playing fields, but, with that exception, includes all land that forms or is to form part of the school premises.

**School Grounds.** School grounds means the playground, school garden and surrounds, and the roads, paths, boundary walls and fences on the school site.

**School Buildings.** The school buildings (*d*) mean any building or part of a building forming part of the school premises, except the buildings described as 'other buildings'.

**Other Buildings.** Other buildings (*e*) mean any building or part of any building forming part of the school premises, required **only** (i) as a caretaker's dwelling, (ii) for use in connection with the playing fields, (iii) for medical inspection and treatment by the local education authority, (iv) for use in providing milk, meals or other refreshment for pupils attending the school.

11

## NOTES

(*a*) **School Premises.** – This term is defined in S.114 (1) of the Education Act, 1944.

(*b*) **Teacher's dwelling-house.** – In the definition of school premises in S.114 (1), a teacher's dwelling-house is excluded from the school premises, except where otherwise expressly provided in the Education Act, 1944. The only case in which the teacher's dwelling-house is expressly included occurs in §8 of the Second Schedule to the Education Act, 1944. That schedule deals with the transfer of the premises of a voluntary school to a local education authority. See, however, Chapter VII, §3, concerning the dwelling-house of the housemaster of a school boarding house.

(*c*) **Site.** – This term is defined in S.16 (1) of the Education Act, 1946.

(*d*) **School Buildings.** – School buildings are defined in S.4 (2) of the Education Act, 1946.

(*e*) **Other Buildings.** – This is a convenient term, used throughout the text of this book, to define all the buildings or parts of buildings, which, by S.4 (2) of the Education Act, 1946, are excluded from the definition of school buildings.

## 3. *References to the Education Acts, 1944 to 1967*

Throughout the following text and notes, references to the sections and schedules of the Education Act, 1944, are given in ordinary type, thus: S.103. References to sections and schedules of the Education Act, 1946, are given in italics, thus: *S.4 (2)*. References to sections of subsequent Education Acts are followed by the title of the Act. Any references to the Education Act, 1944, that is marked with an asterisk, thus: S.15 (3)*, means that the particular provision of the 1944 Act has been amended by subsequent enactments.

# II. THE CONTROLLED SCHOOL

## 1. *Capital Expenditure on School Premises*

In practice, the Education Acts may involve capital expenditure on controlled schools in one of the four following ways: **1** the alteration of the premises of an existing school; **2** the transfer of an existing school to a new site; **3** the enlargement of an existing school to the extent of establishing a new school, in a wide variety of cases; **4** the establishment of a new controlled school in new premises, in replacement of approximately the same accommodation surrendered by the closure or reorganization of existing voluntary schools, or, in the case of the establishment of a new controlled middle school in new premises, in replacement of about the same accommodation surrendered by the closure or reorganization of existing voluntary and county schools.

The provisions of the Acts for each of the four cases are given below:

### (1) Alteration of an Existing Controlled School

The local education authority are responsible for the whole of the expenditure on alterations (*a*) to the premises of a controlled school. Such expenditure may include an addition (*b*) to the existing site, an improvement (*c*) of it, the improvement of the school grounds (*d*), frontagers' road charges, the provision or extension of playing fields (*e*), the provision of any buildings (*f*), or the improvement of the existing buildings (*g*). The authority may carry out all this work (*h*).

The authority must convey their interest in any addition to the existing site, and in any buildings thereon, which are to form part of the school premises, to the trustees of the school (*i*); but the legitimate interests of the authority are protected in the event of the discontinuance of the school by the managers or governors (*j*), and if part or the whole of the premises conveyed to the trustees by the authority are acquired from the trustees by any person (*k*).

The authority are also responsible for meeting any continuing liabilities of the managers or governors (*l*) or their predecessors or the trustees in respect of the provision of the existing premises or equipment for the purposes of the school, but not for any of their previous debts which they may have neglected to pay.

Any playing fields provided by the authority and any buildings provided by the authority on such playing fields, for use in connection therewith, remain the property of the authority (*m*).

### (2) Transfer of an Existing Controlled School to a New Site and Disposal of Old School Premises

If an existing controlled school has to be transferred to a new site (*n*), the authority must meet the cost of the new site, and of the school grounds, of any road charges, and of the school buildings and other buildings of the new premises (*o*), and must provide the playing fields and any buildings on them ($p$). The authority may carry out all this work ($q$). The authority must also convey their interest in the new site and the new school buildings to the trustees of the school ($r$), to be held by them on trust for the purposes of the school; but the playing fields provided by the authority and any buildings on them provided by the authority, for use in connection therewith, remain the property of the authority ($s$).

The authority's legitimate interests are protected in the event of the discontinuance of the school by the managers or governors ($t$), and if part or the whole of the premises are acquired from the trustees by any person ($u$).

Having provided the new site and the new buildings on it which become the property of the trustees, the authority become entitled to part or the whole of the sale proceeds of the old school premises ($v$).

The authority are responsible for meeting any continuing liabilities of the managers or governors ($w$), or their predecessors, or the trustees, in respect of the provision of the old school premises or equipment for the purposes of that school; but the authority are not responsible for any previous debts which the managers or governors may have neglected to pay.

### (3) Enlargement of an Existing Controlled School to the extent of establishing a New School

An existing controlled school may be enlarged to such an extent as to amount to the establishment of a new school ($x$). Subject to certain conditions, such enlargements may be carried out in a wide variety of circumstances ($y$), and the Secretary of State may direct that the expenditure involved shall be payable by the authority ($z$). That expenditure will include the cost of all necessary alterations and additions ($a^1$) to the premises. The authority must also provide the playing fields and any buildings on them ($b^1$). The authority may carry out all this work ($c^1$).

The authority need not convey their interest ($d^1$) in any addition to the existing site, or in any buildings on it that are to form part of the school premises, to the trustees of the school but, in certain circumstances, it may be to their advantage to do so ($e^1$). The playing fields provided by the authority and any buildings on them provided by the authority, for use in connection therewith, remain the property of the authority ($f^1$).

The legitimate interests of the authority are protected in the event of the discontinuance of the school by the managers or governors ($g^1$).

The authority are also responsible for meeting any continuing liabilities of the managers or governors ($h^1$), or their predecessors or trustees, in respect of the provision of the existing school premises and equipment for the purposes of the school, but not for any of their previous debts which they may have neglected to pay.

### (4) Establishment of a New Controlled School in New Premises provided by the Local Education Authority

A new controlled school may be established in new premises ($i^1$) and the authority may meet the whole, or a special part, of the cost incurred, if the new controlled school is required for the purpose of providing accommodation for pupils for whom accommodation would have been provided in some other voluntary school if that other school had not been discontinued, or had not otherwise ceased to be available for the purpose. Additionally, if the new controlled school is to be a middle school ($j^1$), it may be so established for the purpose of providing accommodation for pupils for a substantial proportion of whom accommodation would have been provided in some other voluntary school if that other school had not been discontinued, or had not otherwise ceased to be available for the purpose. The authority may carry out the whole of the work for which they pay ($k^1$). The new premises will normally remain the property of the authority ($l^1$). The playing fields provided by the authority and any buildings on them provided by the authority for use in connection therewith remain the property of the authority ($m^1$).

The legitimate interests of the authority are protected in the event of the discontinuance of the school by the managers or governors ($n^1$).

### NOTES

(a) **Alterations.** – By S.114 (1)* alterations to school premises include improvements, enlargements, or additions, which do not amount to the establishment of a new school (see S.67 (4)). The duty of the L.E.A. to maintain a controlled school, as defined in S.114 (2), includes expenditure on alterations by virtue of S.15 (3).

(b) **Addition.** – By *S.3* and *§1 of the First Schedule* it is the duty of the L.E.A. to provide an addition to the site of a controlled school.

(c) **Improvement.** – The improvement of the site of a controlled school, *e.g.* the making of a playground, is part of the alterations – see note (a) above.

(d) **School grounds.** – See Chapter I, §2.

(e) **Playing fields.** – The duty of the L.E.A. to provide the playing fields of a controlled school is implicit in their obligation to maintain the school – see S.114 (2) – and the *Standards For School Premises Regulations, 1959*, prescribe the provision to be made.

(f) **Any buildings.** – The duty of the L.E.A. to provide any buildings is contained in *S.3* and *§1 of the First Schedule.*

(g) **Improvement of the existing buildings.** – This is part of the alterations – see note (a) above.

(h) **Authority may carry out all this work** by virtue of *S.6.*

(i) **Trustees of the school.** – The obligation of the L.E.A. to convey their interest in any addition to the existing site of a controlled school and in any buildings provided thereon which are to form part of the school premises, is laid down by *S.3* and §6 *of the First Schedule*, which also provides that the Secretary of State shall decide, in case of doubt or dispute, as to the persons to whom the conveyance shall be made.

(j) **Discontinuance of the school by the managers or governors.** – The legitimate interests of the L.E.A. in respect of capital expenditure incurred by them on the premises, are protected by S.14 (1)*, in the event of the discontinuance of the school by the managers or governors.

(k) **If part or the whole of the premises conveyed to the trustees by the authority are acquired from the trustees by any person.** – The legitimate interests of the L.E.A. in respect of capital expenditure incurred by them on the premises of a controlled school conveyed to the trustees by the L.E.A. are protected by *S.3* and §8 *of the First Schedule*, if part or the whole of such premises, or any interest therein, are acquired, whether compulsorily or otherwise from the trustees by any person.

(l) **Continuing liabilities of the managers or governors.** – From the date on which the school becomes a controlled school, any continuing liabilities of the managers or governors, or their predecessors or trustees, in respect of the provision of the existing school premises and equipment for the purposes of the school, are included in the expenditure to be borne by the L.E.A. in maintaining the school. – See S.114 (2) and S.15 (3)*.

(m) **Playing fields remain the property of the authority.** – Playing fields provided by the L.E.A. and any buildings on them provided by the L.E.A. for use in connection therewith, remain the property of the L.E.A. by virtue of their exclusion from the definition of site in *S.16 (1)*.

(*n*) **Transferred to a new site.** – The conditions under which an existing controlled school may be transferred to a new site are set out in S.16 (1); namely, because it is not reasonably practicable to alter the existing premises to conform with the standards prescribed under the Act, or because of any movement of population, or because of any action taken or proposed to be taken under the Housing Acts or the Town and Country Planning Acts. For definition of site see Chapter I, §2.

(*o*) **New Premises.** – All this expenditure must be borne by the L.E.A. by *S.3* and §*1 of the First Schedule.*

(*p*) **Playing fields and any buildings on them.** – See notes (*e*) and ( *f* ) above.

(*q*) **Authority may carry out all this work.** – As to buildings on the new site, by virtue of *S.6*; as to playing fields and buildings on them, because they are provided by and remain the property of the authority.

(*r*) **Trustees of the school.** – The obligation of the L.E.A. to convey their interest in the new site and new buildings on it is laid down by *S.3* and §*6 of the First Schedule.* If there is an existing trust deed, a copy may be available locally, or at the diocesan office or headquarters of the voluntary body concerned, or may be obtained from the Department of Education and Science, or the Public Record Office. If there is no trust deed, or if any doubt or dispute arises as to the persons to whom the L.E.A. are required to convey their interest, the appointment of trustees is to be determined by the Secretary of State, who may make an order under the Charities Act, 1960, after the issue of statutory notices by the legal branch of the Department. In this connection, in the case of a C. of E. controlled school, if the managers or governors or acting trustees, wish to make any representations to the Secretary of State they are first required by the Diocesan Education Committees Measure, 1955, to consult the Diocesan Education Committee, and to have regard to the representations made to them by that Committee. When it is clear who the school trustees are, it is for them to prepare the draft conveyance of the new site and new school buildings from the L.E.A. to themselves. §*6 of the First Schedule* requires that the property conveyed shall be held by the trustees on trust for the purposes of the school. A simple form of conveyance and declaration of trust are all that is required. Although there is no obligation to submit the draft conveyance to the Department, the two parties may prefer to do so, and to lodge a completed copy of the conveyance with the Department. In many instances, the question of sale proceeds of the old premises of the school will also arise – see note (*v*) below; and although the conveyance of the new site and new school buildings must at least immediately precede the handing over of any sale proceeds of the old premises to the L.E.A., it is an advantage, where possible, to deal with any questions about sale proceeds at the same time.

(*s*) **Playing fields . . . remain the property of the authority.** – See note (*m*) above.

(*t*) **Discontinuance of school by managers or governors.** – See note (*j*) above.

(*u*) **If part or the whole of the premises are acquired from the trustees by any person.** – See note (*k*) above.

(*v*) **Sale proceeds of the old school premises.** – If the trustees of the transferred controlled school premises possess, or are or may become entitled to, any sum representing sale proceeds of the old premises of the school, they, or their successors, must pay to the L.E.A. so much of the sum as the Secretary of State may determine to be just having regard to the value of the new property conveyed by the L.E.A. to the trustees. That is required by §*7 of the First Schedule.* The Secretary of State has to frank the figure at which the old premises are sold. A sale, or a lease for more than twenty-two years, requires the consent of the Secretary of State under S.29 of the Charities Act, 1960, and the application to him should be accompanied by a report from a competent surveyor, acting exclusively in the interests of the foundation, deposing to the value of the property. In the great majority of cases, the sale proceeds will be less than the value of the new property conveyed by the L.E.A. to the trustees. In such cases, the L.E.A. will be paid the whole of the net proceeds of the sale of the old school premises. If, however, the old premises fetch more than the value of the new property, the L.E.A. will be recouped for their expenditure in providing the new property conveyed to the trustees, and the balance of the sale proceeds will be retained by the trustees. In some instances, the L.E.A. may have a use for the old premises, if not for education for some other service of the council, in which case, if the trustees and L.E.A. agree, it will normally be possible to arrange for the old premises to be conveyed to the L.E.A. instead of their being sold and the sale proceeds paid to the L.E.A. The trustees must obtain the consent of the Department of Education and Science to such a conveyance, which will be authorized by an order made under S.29 of the Charities Act, 1960. If, in the unusual case, the old premises are worth more than the new property conveyed to the trustees by the L.E.A., the difference will have to be paid by the L.E.A. to the trustees. If the trustees, instead of selling the old premises of the school, lease them at a figure acceptable to the Secretary of State, the net rental will normally be payable to the L.E.A., as provided by the definition of 'sale' in §7 *of the First Schedule*. Some schools are held on trusts which are not solely educational, and are only under the jurisdiction of the Secretary of State so long as the premises are used for school purposes. In such cases, when new premises are provided for the transfer of a controlled school to a new site, the old premises may come under the jurisdiction of the Charity Commissioners, in which event any questions arising or consents required under the Charities Act, 1960, will be dealt with by them and not by the Secretary of State.

Special attention is drawn to the following type of case. In *Attorney-General v. Price* (1912), the dispute was about an elementary school at Caerphilly, held on trust under the School Sites Acts, and the use to which the premises could be put when the school was closed. The case, known as the *Caerphilly Case*, went to the House of Lords, but no judgment was given there because the two parties reached an agreed compromise. The compromise was that so long as the premises were not used as an elementary school, they should be used primarily for C. of E. educational purposes, and secondarily for other educational purposes determined by the trustees. From the time of that case, when elementary schools, held on trust under the School Sites Acts for the purpose of a school, were closed, and a reversioner did not appear, or was unknown, or made no claim, it was the custom of the Board of Education, on application by the persons interested, to make a scheme under the Charitable Trusts Acts, for the premises to be used generally on the lines of the compromise agreed in the *Caerphilly Case*. That practice of the Board of Education came to an end in 1939. Since then, the Board and their successors have declined to make any such schemes. But the assumption that a Caerphilly type of scheme for an alternative use of the old premises of a transferred controlled school might, or would, be made, and that sale proceeds would therefore not be payable to the L.E.A., has led to some misunderstandings which could have been avoided at the outset if it had been generally known that, since 1939, no such schemes would be sanctioned. Another sort of case has led to different misunderstandings about the old premises of transferred controlled schools. When development plans were prepared by L.E.A.s under the Education Act, 1944, they included a list of schools proposed for closure. That did not mean that the schools would, in fact, be closed, but only that it was thought at the time that they would be. The actual closure of a school depends on a specific approval by the Secretary of State under S.13, and in many cases it has been found that circumstances have changed since the development plans were prepared, and that the schools could not be closed. Meanwhile, schemes were made under S.86 to vest the premises of C. of E. schools, proposed in development plans for closure, in the Diocesan Board of Finance, so that, when the schools closed, the sale proceeds could be used for aided schools in the diocese. If, however, a school included in such a scheme was, or afterwards became, a controlled school, which, instead of being closed, had, or has, to be transferred to a new site, then, in spite of the original intention when the school was included in a scheme made under S.86, the sale proceeds of the old premises may be payable instead to the L.E.A. by virtue of §7 *of the First Schedule*. The question should be taken up by the L.E.A. with the Secretary of State and the Diocesan Board of Finance as soon as possible, when the decision is made to transfer the controlled school to a new site. In the following instances, no sale proceeds of the old premises of a transferred controlled school will normally be payable to the L.E.A.: (i) where the old premises do not belong to the trustees of the new premises, *e.g.* the old premises are privately owned; (ii) where the existing trust deed specifically provides that the old premises, on ceasing to be used for the purposes of a school, may be used for other purposes; (iii) where the existing trust deed provides that the old premises, on ceasing to be used for the purposes of a school, may be claimed by a reversioner, and such a claim is exercised.

B CVS

(*w*) **Continuing liabilities of managers or governors.** – See note (*l*) above.

(*x*) **New School.** – Any question as to whether a proposed enlargement constitutes the establishment of a new school is determined by the Secretary of State under S.67 (4). If the enlargement provides accommodation for an increase in the number of pupils of more than 25 per cent, it will be regarded as the establishment of a new school and a proposal will be necessary under S.13. Otherwise, the proposal will be dealt with as the alteration of an existing school. See Chapter II, §1 (1).

(*y*) **Such enlargements may be carried out in a wide variety of circumstances.** – *S.1* as amended by S.3 of the Education (Miscellaneous Provisions) Act, 1953, and again by S.2 of the Education Act, 1967, permits the enlargement of a controlled school, to the extent of establishing a new school, in the following circumstances:

(i) to provide for the closure or reorganization of one or more voluntary schools and for the transfer of the pupils concerned to the enlarged controlled school. This kind of enlargement can take place at a primary school or a secondary school. The enlargement must be wholly or mainly required to provide accommodation for pupils who would have been accommodated in some other voluntary school but for its closure, or for its having ceased to be available to them by reason of reorganization or otherwise. There must be a surrender of voluntary school accommodation elsewhere, but the enlargement may be greater than the amount of voluntary school accommodation surrendered, because a county school, in addition, can be included in the arrangement. That is to say, a county school can be closed or reorganized, and the equivalent of its accommodation thereby surrendered can be included in the enlargement of the controlled school, provided that the enlargement is mainly for the transfer of voluntary school pupils, and the county school pupils are a minority of those to be transferred to the enlarged controlled school;

(ii) *either* because the enlargement of the controlled school is desirable for the better provision of primary or secondary education at the premises to be enlarged, *or* for securing that there is available for the area of the L.E.A. a sufficiency of suitable primary or secondary schools, *or* for both those reasons. It is in these respects that S.2 of the Education Act, 1967, has removed the limiting provisions of *S.1* as amended by S.3 of the 1953 Act. Under the latter, this kind of enlargement was only allowed in the case of secondary schools, and then was limited by the two following conditions: (*a*) that the enlargement of the controlled secondary school was kept within reasonable limits, for example from two-form entry to three-form entry, because, to quote the Minister during the passage of the 1953 Bill, it would be contrary to the settlement embodied in the 1944 Act to permit the use of this section to enlarge a controlled school to a considerable degree at the public expense; (*b*) that the enlargement was not likely to amount to the establishment of a secondary school of a new character, *e.g.* the establishment of a comprehensive school by enlarging a grammar school. The limitations of *S.1*, as amended by the 1953 Act, having been removed by the 1967 Act it is now possible in planning the expansion of school accommodation, and in dealing with reorganization schemes involving the establishment of primary schools, or of middle schools, junior high schools, comprehensive schools, and sixth form colleges, to consider the resources of controlled and county schools together in an area, and, if it seems desirable, to enlarge a controlled school to the extent required, and to change its character, to fit the plan or scheme desired. In other words, the 1967 Act allows great flexibility in dealing with the enlargement of a controlled school.

In proposing the enlargement of a controlled school to the extent of establishing a new school, the L.E.A. and the managers or governors of the controlled school must each apply to the Secretary of State for his approval, and approval under S.13 is also required. Unless both parties have made the above-mentioned application to him, the Secretary of State cannot direct the L.E.A. to meet the cost of enlarging a controlled school to the extent of establishing a new school. On the other hand, in some circumstances, any solution other than such an enlargement might involve a proposal or proposals under S.13 for the establishment of a new school or schools that would be altogether unrealistic, and fail to obtain approval by the Secretary of State.

An enlargement of a controlled school to the extent of establishing a new school can only be carried out on the site of the existing school, or on an addition to the site. But see note ($e^1$) below.

($z$) **The expenditure involved shall be payable by the authority.** – *S.1* (and as amended by S.3 of the 1953 Act and by S.2 of the 1967 Act) provides that upon a joint application by the L.E.A. and the managers or governors, the Secretary of State may by order direct that the expenditure shall be payable by the L.E.A.

($a^1$) **And additions.** – Additions are included in the enlargement by virtue of *S.1 (2)*.

($b^1$) **Playing fields and buildings on them.** – See notes ($e$) and ($f$) above.

($c^1$) **Authority may carry out all this work.** – As to buildings, by virtue of *S.6*, which, because of S.20 (3) of the Education (Miscellaneous Provisions) Act, 1953, also applies to an enlargement carried out under S.3 of that Act; as to playing fields and buildings on them, because they are provided by and remain the property of the L.E.A.

($d^1$) **The authority need not convey their interest.** – It is important to notice several matters in connection with the enlargement of a controlled school under *S.1*. First, the L.E.A. acquire no interest in the sale proceeds of the premises of any voluntary school that is discontinued on the transfer of pupils to the enlarged controlled school. Secondly, as the enlarged controlled school is a new school, the provisions of §7 *of the First Schedule* do not apply. The L.E.A. may, therefore, retain the ownership of any addition they provide to the existing site and of any buildings they provide thereon. Thirdly, as the enlarged controlled school is a new school, the provisions of §8 *of the First Schedule* do not apply.

Where the L.E.A. retain the ownership, it may be necessary, in order that the new controlled school shall have a trust deed for the purposes desired by the proposers, for a lease to trustees to be arranged. See note ($l^1$) below.

($e^1$) **It may be to their advantage to do so.** – In a case, for example, where a controlled school is enlarged to the extent of establishing a new school, by building on a new site (as an addition to the existing site) to be followed subsequently by further building on the new site to replace the old premises, thereby securing that the whole of the premises of the new school comply with the standards of the 1944 Act, the Secretary of State will regard the land on which the first new building – for the enlargement – takes place, as an addition to the existing site; and he will not regard the building of the second instalment – to replace the old buildings – as a transfer of the school to a new site under S.16 (1). Instead, he will regard it as an alteration of the enlarged school to conform with the standards of the 1944 Act. In such a case, it will normally be to the advantage of the L.E.A. to obtain the sale proceeds of the old premises as an offset to their expenditure on the new. That can be secured, where the premises are vested in trustees, as a condition of agreeing to a joint application with the managers or governors to the Secretary of State under *S.1* as amended by S.3 of the Education (Miscellaneous Provisions) Act, 1953, and by S.2 of the Education Act, 1967, for the enlargement of the school, *i.e.* the trustees will subsequently convey the old premises, free of cost to the L.E.A., if the L.E.A. will vest the new site and the new school buildings, when completed, in the trustees. The Secretary of State will approve an agreement between the L.E.A. and the trustees to that effect, always assuming, of course, that the sale proceeds of the old premises are less than the cost to the L.E.A. of providing the new site and the new school buildings.

($f^1$) **Remain the property of the authority.** – By virtue of their exclusion from the definition of site in *S.16 (1)*.

($g^1$) **Discontinuance of the school by the managers or governors.** – Either because the premises belong to the L.E.A., or, where they have been conveyed to the school trustees, by virtue of S.14 (1)*.

($h^1$) **Continuing liabilities of the managers or governors.** – See note ($l$) above.

($i^1$) **New controlled school may be established in new premises.** – S.2 of the Education (Miscellaneous Provisions) Act, 1953, enables a new controlled school to be established in new premises paid for wholly, or in part, by the L.E.A. This provision is intended to deal with cases in which it is impossible to enlarge an existing controlled school to the extent of establishing a new school – see Chapter II, §1 (3) above. Such cases arise (i) where it is desirable to establish a new controlled school in substitution for other voluntary schools to be discontinued, and/or (ii) to provide for the reorganization of other voluntary schools by the transfer of some of their pupils to a new school. The accommodation of the new controlled school must, broadly speaking, correspond to the accommodation surrendered in the other voluntary schools to be closed or reorganized. The correspondence need not be exact, *i.e.* the new accommodation may be rounded off to a convenient class or form-entry size, if that can be done without conflict with the above-mentioned main purpose. In that event, some spare places will be available for other pupils, including, possibly, pupils from a county school. But it is not possible to use S.2 of the 1953 Act to establish a new controlled school with the object of providing for the closure or reorganization of county schools as well as voluntary schools, except in the special case of a middle school, referred to in note (*j*¹) below.

The proposers and the L.E.A. must satisfy the Secretary of State that the above-mentioned conditions will be fulfilled, and the proposal also requires his approval under S.13. If the Secretary of State approves the proposal he may make an order directing that the whole, or a special part, of the cost in establishing the new controlled school shall be met by the L.E.A. In most cases the L.E.A. will meet the whole cost – see note (*l*¹) below.

If the L.E.A. and the proposers do not agree to the establishment of a new controlled school in new premises, then whether the proposal relates to a primary school, or a secondary school, or a middle school, it will normally fall to the ground. On the other hand, in some circumstances, the alternative to such a proposal might involve a different proposal under S.13 that would be unrealistic and fail to obtain the approval of the Secretary of State.

(*j*¹) **If the new controlled school is to be a middle school.** – If the new controlled school is to be a middle school, it may be established in substitution for other voluntary school accommodation, as described in note (*i*¹) above. But, by the amendment of S.2 of the Education (Miscellaneous Provisions) Act, 1953, made by S.3 of the Education Act, 1967, a new controlled middle school may also be established in substitution for the surrender of both county and voluntary school accommodation, provided that a substantial proportion of the pupils for whom the new school is established are from voluntary schools. It is not required that the pupils from the voluntary schools shall be in a majority, though that may normally prove to be the case. So the amendment made by S.3 of the 1967 Act, if the proposers and the L.E.A. agree, allows a good deal of flexibility to them. The exceptional treatment thus afforded for the establishment of new controlled middle schools stems from the fact that, by now, schools have been reorganized as separate primary and secondary schools, with the usual dividing age between the two stages. A middle school, however, defined in S.1 of the Education Act, 1964, straddles the normal dividing age between primary and secondary schools. The establishment of a middle school therefore involves taking pupils from at least two schools, one primary and one secondary. In the absence of S.3 of the Education Act, 1967, there would be less scope for the establishment of new controlled middle schools than was already afforded by S.2 of the 1953 Act, for the establishment of other kinds of controlled schools.

(*k*¹) **Authority may carry out the whole of the work for which they pay.** – As to buildings, by virtue of *S.6*, which, because of S.20 (3) of the Education (Miscellaneous Provisions) Act, 1953, also applies to the building of a controlled school under S.2 of the latter Act; as to playing fields and buildings on them for use in connection therewith, because they are provided by and remain the property of the L.E.A.

(*l*¹) **The new premises will normally remain the property of the authority.** – In most cases in which a new controlled school is established in new premises, the order made by the Secretary of State under S.2 of the Education (Miscellaneous Provisions) Act, 1953, as amended by the 1967 Act, will provide that the L.E.A. shall meet the whole cost of establishing the new school. That will be so because, if the resources (if any) of the proposers are so slender that they cannot establish a new aided school instead, with the grant of 80 per cent from the Secretary of State and the facilities available to them of a loan, the L.E.A. may prefer to meet the whole cost and retain the premises as their property, as they are entitled to do. In that event, if the proposers desire that the managers or governors of the new controlled school shall be able to arrange for denominational religious instruction to be given in the school, during not more than two periods a week, to children whose parents request it, then, as the school is a new school, it will need to have a trust deed for that purpose – see S.27 and Chapter II, §4. A solution to the problem can be found by the L.E.A.'s granting a long lease of the new site and school buildings, as property to be held on trust, at a nominal rent, to persons appointed as school trustees, such a lease providing that the trust property shall not be used for any purpose other than that of a controlled school – see S.22 – and that the L.E.A. shall have an unencumbered freehold of the property if the school should be closed. Such a lease would include the necessary provision, mentioned above, regarding denominational religious instruction. The consent of the Secretary of State is not required to such a lease.

($m^1$) **Remain the property of the authority.** – By virtue of S.13 (7)* the authority must provide the playing fields and any buildings on them, and the Education Acts do not require the L.E.A. to convey them to trustees.

($n^1$) **Discontinuance of the school by the managers or governors.** – Either because the L.E.A. have retained the ownership of the new premises, or by S.14 (1)*.

# 2. Instrument and Rules of Management of a Controlled Primary School

The instrument of management (a) of a controlled primary school, which provides for the constitution of the body of managers, is made by an order of the Secretary of State (b). Subject to a minimum of six managers, the number will be determined by the Secretary of State, after consultation with the local education authority (c). If there are six managers, they will be appointed as follows: in a county, two foundation managers (d), two L.E.A., two minor authority (e); in a county borough, two foundation, four L.E.A.; if there are nine managers, as follows: in a county, three foundation, four L.E.A., two minor authority; or three foundation, three L.E.A., three minor authority; in a county borough, three foundation, six L.E.A.

The rules of management (f) are made by an order of the authority. These rules govern the conduct of the school, subject to the provisions of the Education Acts (g), and of any trust deed of the school (h). If the Secretary of State considers that anything included or proposed to be included in the instrument or rules of management is inconsistent with the trust deed, and if he thinks it just and expedient, in the interests of the school, that the trust deed should be modified (i) to remove the inconsistency, he may make an order modifying the trust deed (j). But before doing so, he is bound to give an opportunity to the authority, and to any other persons who appear to him to be concerned with the management of the school, to make representations to him; and he must also have regard to all the circumstances of the school and, in the case of an existing school, to the manner in which it has previously been conducted.

Specimen instrument and rules of management for a controlled primary school are given in the Appendix.

## NOTES

(a) **Instrument of management.** – See S.17 (1). The Instrument, besides fixing the constitution and method of appointment of the managers, in accordance with the provisions of the Education Acts, also regulates the proceedings of the managers in accordance with S.21 and the Fourth Schedule as amended by the Education (Miscellaneous Provisions) Act, 1948. Special provision for the grouping of two or more schools under one managing body may be made with the consent of the voluntary school managers. For details of such special arrangements see S.20.

Apart from certain matters specifically reserved for determination by or reference to the Foundation Managers, relating to denominational religious instruction, appointment and dismissal of reserved teachers, and the use to which the school premises may be put on Sundays – see Chapter II, §§4, 6, 8 – all matters coming within the purview of the managers stand referred to the whole of the managers. – See note to §18 of Specimen Instrument of Management given in the Appendix.

(b) **Order of the Secretary of State.** – See S.17 (2).

(c) **After consultation with the local education authority.** – See S.18 (3). The consultation will usually be limited to the consideration of the reasons, if any, why the number of managers should be more than six. The number of managers must be a multiple of three.

(d) **Foundation managers** are defined in S.114 (1)* as persons appointed otherwise than by a L.E.A. or minor authority, for the purpose of securing, so far as is practicable, that the character of the school as a voluntary school is preserved and developed, and, in particular, that the school is conducted in accordance with the provisions of any trust deed of the school.

(e) **Minor authority.** – See the definition in S.114 (1)*. In a county area the minor authority is the council of a non-county borough, or urban district, or rural parish, which appears to the L.E.A. to be the area served by the school. If the area is a rural parish for which there is no parish council, the parish meeting will be the minor authority; and where the L.E.A. consider that the school serves the area of two or more minor authorities, the minor authority for the purpose of appointing managers is to be all those minor authorities acting jointly. If a school is closed and the pupils are transferred to a school in a different parish, then if the area of the latter school is extended, the Secretary of State must make a variation order so as to amend its instrument of management to include the additional parish in the minor authority. In the Inner London Area, the minor authority is the council of the inner London borough, or the Common Council of the City of London, whose area appears to the I.L.E.A. to be served by the school – see The London Government Act, 1963, S.31 (10). In a county borough, there is no minor authority, and in such an area, the L.E.A. will appoint all the managers who are not foundation managers. – See S.18 (3) (c).

(f) **Rules of management.** – See S.17 (3) (a).

(g) **Subject to the provisions of the Education Acts.** – By S.17 (3) the rules must be made by the L.E.A. Obviously they must not conflict with the provisions of the Acts.

(h) **And of any trust deed of the school.** – Trust deed is defined in S.114 (1)* as including any instrument (not being an instrument of management or rules of management made under the Education Act, 1944) regulating the maintenance, management or conduct of the school or the constitution of the body of managers thereof.

(i) **That the trust deed should be modified.** – The trust deed drawn up before the passage of the Education Act, 1944, may require modification so that it does not conflict with the statutory provisions of the new Act.

(j) **Order modifying the trust deed.** – S.17 (4) gives this necessary power to the Secretary of State and S.17 (5) closely prescribes the procedure to be followed before exercising it. The statutory provisions of the Act, the interests of the school, and the manner in which it has been conducted in the past are the three factors governing any modifications of a trust deed.

# 3. *Instrument and Articles of Government of a Controlled Secondary School*

The instrument of government (a) of a controlled secondary school, which provides for the constitution of the body of governors, is made by an order of the Secretary of State (b). The number of governors is determined by the Secretary of State after consultation with the local education authority, but one-third must be foundation governors (c) and two-thirds must be governors appointed by the authority (d).

The articles of government (e) are made by an order of the Secretary of State. These articles govern the conduct of the school, subject to the provisions of the Education Acts and of any trust deed of the school (f), and the articles must, in particular, define the functions to be exercised by the authority, the governors and the head teacher. If the Secretary of

State considers that anything included or proposed to be included in the instrument or articles of government is inconsistent with the trust deed and if he thinks it just and expedient, in the interests of the school, that the trust deed should be modified (g) to remove the inconsistency, he may make an order modifying the trust deed. But before doing so, he is bound to give an opportunity to the authority, and to any other persons who appear to him to be concerned with the government of the school, to make representations to him; and he must also have regard to all the circumstances of the school and, in the case of an existing school, to the manner in which it has previously been conducted.

Specimen instrument and articles of government are given in the Appendix.

## NOTES

(a) **Instrument of government.** – See S.17 (1). The instrument, besides fixing the constitution and the method of appointment of the governors, in accordance with the provisions of the Education Acts, also regulates the proceedings of the governors in accordance with S.21 and the Fourth Schedule as amended by the Education (Miscellaneous Provisions) Act, 1948.

Special provision for the grouping of two or more schools under one governing body may be made with the consent of the governors of a voluntary school. For details of such arrangements see S.20.

Apart from certain matters specifically reserved for reference to or determination by the foundation governors, relating to denominational religious instruction, appointment and dismissal of reserved teachers, and the use to which the school premises may be put on Sundays – see Chapter II, §§4, 6, 8 – all matters coming within the purview of the governors stand referred to the whole of the governors. – See note to §18 of Specimen Instrument of Management (Government) given in the Appendix.

(b) **Order of the Secretary of State.** – See S.17 (2).

(c) **Foundation governors.** – See S.19 (2) (a). See also Chapter II, §2, note (d). The same provisions apply to foundation governors.

(d) **Governors appointed by the authority.** – See S.19 (2) (b). The total number of foundation and authority governors must be a multiple of three.

(e) **Articles of government.** – See S.17 (3) (b). The general policy of the Secretary of State regarding the Instrument and Articles of Government of maintained county and voluntary secondary schools was set out in a White Paper entitled *The Principles of Government in Maintained Secondary Schools* presented to Parliament in 1944 (Cmd. 6523), and obtainable from H.M. Stationery Office.

(f) **Trust deed of the school.** – Trust deed is defined in S.114 (1)* as including any instrument (not being an instrument of government, or articles of government made under the Education Act, 1944) regulating the maintenance, management or conduct of the school or the constitution of the body of governors thereof.

(g) **That the trust deed should be modified.** – S.17 (4) gives this necessary power to the Secretary of State and S.17 (5) closely prescribes the procedure to be followed before exercising it. The trust deed drawn up before the passage of the Education Act, 1944, will normally have to be substantially modified or repealed so that it does not conflict with the statutory provisions of the new Act. These provisions, the interests of the school, and the manner in which it has been conducted in the past, are the three factors to which regard must be paid in modifying the trust deed.

# 4. *Religious Worship and Religious Instruction in a Controlled School*

The school day in a controlled school must begin with collective worship (a) for all pupils except those who have been withdrawn (b) from such worship by their parents. The religious worship must take place on the school premises (c) and, unless the managers or governors consider that the premises make the arrangement impracticable, a single act of worship must be arranged (*d*).

The Education Acts do not specify the character of the religious worship (*e*) in a controlled school, but if the trust deed of the school does, its provisions must be carried out; otherwise, unless the Courts determine to the contrary, it is for the managers or governors to decide whether the religious worship shall be in accordance with the practice observed in the school before it became a controlled school or whether it shall be undenominational in character.

Religious instruction must be given in the school (*f*), but a parent may withdraw his pupil from such instruction (*g*), or may withdraw his pupil from the school in order to receive religious instruction, of a kind which is not provided in the school, elsewhere (*h*).

If the parents of any pupils request that they may receive religious instruction in accordance with the trust deed relating to the school (*i*) or, where provision for that purpose is not made by such a deed, in accordance with the practice observed before the school became a controlled school, the foundation managers or foundation governors must make arrangements (*j*) for such religious instruction to be given to those pupils during not more than two periods (*k*) in each week, unless owing to special circumstances they think it would be unreasonable to make such arrangements (*l*). Apart from such arrangements for the pupils concerned, religious instruction in a controlled school must be given in accordance with an agreed syllabus (*m*).

If a pupil is withdrawn by his parent from religious worship and/or religious instruction in order to receive religious instruction, of a kind which is not provided in the school, elsewhere, the following conditions must be observed (*n*):

(i) the authority must be satisfied that the pupil cannot reasonably attend a school at which the desired religious instruction is given; (ii) the authority must be satisfied that arrangements have, in fact, been made for the pupil to receive the desired religious instruction elsewhere; (iii) the withdrawal of the pupil can only be made either at the beginning or at the end of the school session, and only for such periods as are reasonably necessary.

A pupil must not be required (*o*), as a condition of attending the school either to attend or to abstain from attending a Sunday School or a place or religious worship.

Where religious instruction other than agreed syllabus instruction is arranged for pupils in a controlled school at the request of their parents, only the foundation managers or foundation governors are entitled to make arrangements for the inspection of such instruction (*p*).

The inspection of the agreed syllabus religious instruction (*q*) given in a controlled school may only be carried out by the following persons: (i) one of H.M. Inspectors, (ii) a person appointed by the Secretary of State as an additional inspector and ordinarily employed for the purpose of inspecting secular instruction, (iii) an officer in the full-time employment of the authority who is ordinarily employed for the purpose of inspecting secular instruction.

## NOTES

(*a*) **Must begin with collective worship,** by virtue of S.25 (1).

(*b*) **Except those who have been withdrawn.** – The parent of any pupil may request (preferably, but not necessarily, in writing, to the head teacher, managers or governors, or L.E.A.) that he be wholly or partly excused from attendance at religious worship in the school (see S.25 (4)); such request must be granted and be assumed to continue in force until it is withdrawn by the parent. Following such a request, the pupil may be absent from the worship and be on the school premises, or his parent may send him to school so as to arrive when the worship is over. This provision of the Act is, of course, part of the 'Conscience Clause'. See also note (*g*) below.

(*c*) **Must take place on the school premises,** by virtue of *S.7 (1)*. Although the collective worship must always take place on the school premises, and although a pupil cannot be withdrawn from religious worship in a controlled school to attend religious worship elsewhere, there is, by S.39 (2) (*b*), no obligation on a parent to send his pupil to school on any day exclusively set apart for religious observance by the body to which he belongs. Moreover, the managers, as a body, may resolve that the school shall have an occasional holiday (within the number of days allowed by the L.E.A. for such holidays) on any particular day, *e.g.* Ascension Day.

(*d*) **A single Act of worship must be arranged.** – See S.25 (1).

(*e*) **Character of the religious worship.** – Parliament provided in the Education Act, 1944, that religious instruction in a controlled school shall be in accordance with an agreed syllabus and undenominational, except that trust deed instruction (or instruction in accordance with the practice previously observed), commonly denominational in character, shall be arranged for not more than two periods a week for pupils whose parents ask for such instruction. Thus two different kinds of religious instruction may have to be arranged, but, if religious instruction is given daily, the provision for undenominational instruction will predominate.

Parliament provided for a single act of religious worship, however, but did not specify its character in the Act. As the conduct of the school is under the control of the managers or governors, the position therefore appears to be as follows:

(i) If the trust deed of the school specifies the character of the religious *worship*, then, unless the Secretary of State makes an order modifying the trust deed in that respect the managers or governors must see that its provisions as regards religious worship are carried out.

(ii) If the trust deed of the school does not specify the character of the religious *worship* – and that is usually the case – then, in the absence of a determination by the Courts to the contrary, there appears to be nothing to prevent the managers or governors from arranging that the religious worship shall be in accordance with the practice observed in the school before it became a controlled school, or from arranging that the religious worship shall be undenominational in character.

Reluctance to resort to the Courts to determine between these two alternatives may lead managers or governors to decide to follow the practice previously observed in the school, or to make such adjustments as can readily be accepted by all concerned.

Save as may otherwise be provided by the trust deed, the managers or governors may decide that the act of worship, as an integral part of the activities of the school, shall be conducted by the normal teaching staff of the school; but they may also decide that a clergyman or minister, according to the character of the controlled school, may occasionally conduct the act of worship. Such occasions should be entered in the School Record.

(*f*) **Religious instruction must be given in the school,** by virtue of S.25 (2).

(*g*) **May withdraw his pupil from such instruction,** *i.e.* by requesting that his pupil be wholly or partly excused from attendance at such instruction – S.25 (4). Such a request (made preferably, but not necessarily, in writing, to the head teacher, managers or governors, or L.E.A.) must be granted and be assumed to continue in force until it is withdrawn by the parent. Following such a request, the pupil may be absent from the religious instruction and be on the school premises, or, if the instruction is given at the beginning or end of the school session, the parent may send him to school so as to arrive when the religious instruction has ended, or may insist on his leaving school before it begins. This again is part of the 'Conscience Clause'.

(*h*) **In order to receive religious instruction, of a kind which is not provided in the school, elsewhere.** – Under S.25 (5) a pupil may be withdrawn by his parent from religious worship, or religious instruction, or from both, in order to receive religious instruction, of a kind which is not provided in the school, elsewhere. It follows, for example, that a pupil in a Church of England controlled school may be withdrawn for Roman Catholic or Nonconformist religious instruction elsewhere, but not for Church of England instruction. A possible exception to this might arise if special circumstances made it impossible for the foundation managers or foundation governors to arrange for the trust deed (or previous practice) instruction to be given on the school premises owing to the inadequacy of the present premises (see note (*l*) below). In such exceptional circumstances, if the conditions mentioned below (see note (*n*) and text) were fulfilled, withdrawal might take place. Withdrawal of a pupil from any controlled school to receive agreed syllabus instruction elsewhere cannot take place.

(*i*) **Trust deed relating to the school.** – See S.27 (1). See also Chapter II, §2, note (*h*), and §3, note (*f*). A trust deed may provide for denominational instruction, or, in some cases, for undenominational instruction. S.67 (3) provides that where any trust deed relating to a voluntary school makes provision whereby a bishop or any other ecclesiastical or denominational authority has power to decide whether the religious instruction given in the school which purports to be in accordance with the provisions of the trust deed does or does not accord with those provisions, that question shall be determined in accordance with the provisions of the trust deed.

(*j*) **Foundation managers or foundation governors must make arrangements.** – See Chapter II, §2, note (*d*), and §3, note (*c*). The arrangements for such religious instruction are under the control of the foundation managers or foundation governors subject to any provisions of the trust deed – see S.27 (1).

There is nothing to prevent the foundation managers or governors from letting parents know that they may request that their pupils may have religious instruction in accordance with the trust deed, or, where no such provision is made by such a deed, in accordance with the practice observed in the school before it became a controlled school. It will be appreciated that difficulties can best be avoided by obtaining all such requests in writing.

In a controlled school in which there is no reserved teacher, the arrangements made will probably provide for the instruction to be given by a clergyman or minister, according to the character of the controlled school. There is nothing to prevent the head teacher or a non-reserved assistant teacher (if either of them wish to do so) from giving such religious instruction under the arrangements made by the foundation managers or foundation governors; but it is entirely a matter in the discretion of the head teacher and the non-reserved assistant teacher, respectively, and must have nothing to do with their appointment or their holding office.

(*k*) **Two periods.** – See S.27 (1). This means two periods in the time-table of the school and the requirements of *The Schools Regulations, 1959*, as to the part of the school session devoted to secular instruction must be observed. Two periods a week may be arranged for each class (or group of sufficient size) of pupils whose parents request that they shall have the religious instruction arranged by the foundation managers or foundation governors. If, for example, the L.E.A. arrange the period of secular instruction – see S.23 (1) and Chapter II, §5 – in a primary school so that religious instruction is given each day, the pupils who take denominational instruction will have not less than three periods of agreed syllabus instruction and not more than two periods of denominational instruction a week.

(*l*) **Unreasonable to make such arrangements.** – The special circumstances under which the foundation managers or foundation governors might be satisfied that it would be unreasonable to make arrangements for denominational instruction might include the following: (i) that special difficulties made it impossible for them to arrange for a competent person to give the instruction; (ii) that the managers as a body had arranged for religious instruction to be given each day and the inadequacy of the present school premises made it impracticable for denominational instruction to be given at the same time as the other pupils were receiving agreed syllabus instruction – see also note (*h*) above.

(*m*) **Agreed syllabus.** – See S.29 and the Fifth Schedule. This means the agreed syllabus adopted by the L.E.A. on the unanimous recommendation of the statutory conference consisting of duly appointed representatives of religious denominations, teachers and of the L.E.A. If arrangements cannot be made to secure a unanimous recommendation, or if the L.E.A. fail to adopt any syllabus unanimously recommended to them by the conference, the Secretary of State has the duty to appoint a body of persons having experience in religious instruction to prepare a syllabus of religious instruction to be adopted by the L.E.A. Such a body of persons must, as far as practicable, be of like representative character to the conference appointed by the L.E.A. An agreed syllabus must be undenominational in character.

(*n*) **The following conditions must be observed.** – See S. 25 (5). These conditions are imposed by the Act on all schools.

(*o*) **A pupil must not be required.** – See S. 25 (3). This is the third part of the 'Conscience Clause'. See notes (*b*) and (*g*) above.

(*p*) **Arrangements for the inspection of such instruction.** – See the proviso to S.77 (5). Inspections of such instruction may not be made on more than two days in any year in any voluntary school, and not less than fourteen days' notice of an inspection must be given by the foundation managers or foundation governors to the L.E.A. By S.77 (6) no pupil who has been excused from attendance at religious worship or religious instruction in a voluntary school in accordance with the provisions of the Act (see notes (*b*), (*g*) and (*h*) above) shall be required to attend the school on any day fixed for such inspection.

Only those pupils who are receiving religious instruction otherwise than in accordance with an agreed syllabus may be inspected under the arrangements made by the foundation managers or foundation governors. The foundation managers or foundation governors may, where appropriate, arrange for the inspection of denominational instruction to be carried out by a diocesan inspector.

A day on which the inspection of this religious instruction takes place counts as a day on which the school meets. After the school day has opened with religious worship, the inspection of denominational instruction takes precedence over secular instruction, and the ordinary time-table must give way to the arrangements of the inspector. The inspector's arrangements will presumably include a conference with the teacher or teachers who give the denominational instruction. If the inspection and conference are held and completed during the morning session, the ordinary time-table will be resumed for the afternoon session, unless the managers have arranged that the afternoon shall be taken as a half-day's holiday out of the annual allowance of occasional holidays of the school. If the inspection and conference are held during the afternoon session, or if they are held during the morning and afternoon sessions, the pupils may be allowed to leave school after the inspection, if the inspector's arrangements for his conference with the teacher or teachers who give the denominational instruction so require; otherwise, the ordinary time-table will be resumed for the remainder of the afternoon session.

(*q*) **Inspection of the agreed syllabus religious instruction** may only be carried out by the persons specified, by virtue of S.77 (5).

# 5. *Secular Instruction in a Controlled School*

Except where otherwise provided in the rules of management or articles of government, the secular instruction in a controlled school is under the control of the local education authority (*a*). This control includes the power to determine (*b*) the times of the school sessions, the school terms, and holidays, and to require the attendance at classes in secular instruction held off the school premises. The authority, however, must not give any directions that will interfere with the provision of reasonable facilities for religious instruction (*c*) in the school during school hours; and the authority must not give directions that will prevent a pupil receiving religious instruction during the hours normally set apart for that purpose (*d*), unless arrangements are made for the pupil to receive religious instruction in the school at some other time.

## NOTES

(*a*) **Under the control of the local education authority,** by virtue of S.23 (1). The measure of control delegated to managers, governors, and head teachers is set out in the Rules of Management or Articles of Government, and, in the case of a secondary school, S.17 (3) (*b*) particularly requires that the articles shall determine the functions to be exercised by the L.E.A., the governors, and the head teacher.

The L.E.A. have the right to cause an inspection of any county or voluntary school maintained by them, but such inspections are to be made by officers appointed by the L.E.A. – see S.77 (3). The Secretary of State has also the right to cause inspections of county and voluntary schools by H.M. Inspector or by additional inspectors – see S.77 (2).

(*b*) **Power to determine.** – This power, given under S.23 (3), is to be exercised in accordance with the provisions of the regulations of the Secretary of State, and, in particular, in accordance with *The Schools Regulations, 1959*. The Secretary of State also has the general power under S.68 to determine that the L.E.A. have acted unreasonably and to issue directions accordingly to them.

(*c*) **Reasonable facilities for religious instruction.** – See S.25 (6). The L.E.A. may wish to give facilities for religious instruction each day. This can be done by directing, for example, that the period of secular instruction shall begin not later than half an hour after the beginning of the school session on any school day and shall continue until the end of the school session on that day. Alternatively, if, in any particular case, the managers desire that the period of religious instruction on any school day shall take place at the end of the school session on that day, the L.E.A. could direct that the period of secular instruction shall not be less on any school day than as set out above. Special arrangements could be made by the L.E.A., if necessary, to vary the direction, if for any special reason, the managers of a primary school desired to arrange the period of religious instruction otherwise than at the beginning or end of the school session; but in a school in which facilities are given for religious instruction each day, there is something to be said for a direction under which that instruction is given at the beginning or end of the school session, because of the statutory arrangements for withdrawal from religious instruction (see Chapter II, §4).

The L.E.A. will, no doubt, direct that arrangements must be made to ensure that there is no interference with the periods devoted to religious worship and religious instruction by the registration of attendances, by the collection of money for school meals or savings banks, or by any other school activities.

(*d*) **During the hours normally set apart for such purpose.** – See S.25 (6). If in certain circumstances, *e.g.* organization of a practical class held off the school premises, the usual time-table for religious instruction is disturbed, compensating arrangements must be made.

# 6. *Teachers in a Controlled School*

Subject to the powers of the foundation managers or foundation governors concerning the appointment of reserved teachers, referred to below, the appointment of all teachers in a controlled school will be under the control of the local education authority (*a*), except in so far as such control is delegated to the managers or governors (*b*) under the rules of management or articles of government for the school. No teacher in a controlled school may be dismissed except by the authority (*c*).

Other special and general conditions concerning the appointment and dismissal of teachers in a controlled school are given below.

### (1) Reserved Teachers

A reserved teacher (*d*) is a person selected for his fitness and competence to give religious instruction in accordance with the provisions of the trust deed (or, where provision for that purpose is not made by such a deed, in accordance with the practice observed in the school before it became a controlled school) under the arrangements made by the foundation managers or foundation governors (e) and who is specifically appointed to do so (f).

If the number of the teaching staff (g) of a controlled school does not exceed two, no reserved teachers may be appointed on the staff of that school (h).

If the number of the teaching staff of a controlled school is greater than two, reserved teachers must be appointed on the staff (i) of that school, as follows:—

| Total number of teaching staff | Number of reserved teachers to be included on the staff |
|---|---|
| 3— 5 | 1 |
| 6—10 | 2 |
| 11—15 | 3 |
| 16—20 | 4 |
| etc. | etc. |

The authority must consult the foundation managers or foundation governors (j) before any person is appointed as a reserved teacher in the controlled school, and unless the foundation managers or foundation governors are satisfied that the person is fit and competent to give the required religious instruction (k), the authority must not appoint that person as a reserved teacher in that school (l).

If the foundation managers or foundation governors consider that any reserved teacher has failed to give the required religious instruction efficiently and suitably, they may require the authority to dismiss him from employment as a reserved teacher in that school (m).

## (2) Head Teacher

The head teacher of a controlled school must not, while holding that position (n), be a reserved teacher. Before appointing a person to be the head teacher of a controlled school, the authority must inform the managers or governors of the school whom they propose to appoint, and must consider any representations made by the managers or governors (o) with respect to the proposed appointment.

## (3) General Conditions relating to Non-Reserved Teachers (p)

No person is to be disqualified from being a teacher, other than a reserved teacher, in a controlled school by reason of his religious opinions, or of his attending or omitting to attend religious worship (q). No such teacher (r) shall be required to give religious instruction (s), or receive any less emolument or be deprived of, or disqualified for, any promotion or other advantage by reason of the fact that he does or does not give religious instruction, or by reason of his religious opinions, or of his attending or omitting to attend religious worship.

## (4) General Conditions relating to Reserved Teachers (t)

A reserved teacher shall not receive any less emolument or be deprived of, or disqualified for, any promotion or other advantage by reason of the fact that he gives religious instruction, or by reason of his religious opinions or of his attending religious worship.

### (5) Women Teachers and Marriage

No woman is to be disqualified for employment as a teacher in a controlled school, or be dismissed from such employment, by reason only of marriage (*u*).

#### NOTES

(*a*) **Under the control of the local education authority.** – See S.24 (1). This control is comprehensive, subject to the conditions laid down by the Act. All teachers in a controlled school are officers of the L.E.A. The L.E.A. may fix the number of teachers to be employed in a school, and may appoint the teachers, subject to any powers delegated to the managers or governors under the rules of management or articles of government for the school.

(*b*) **Except in so far as such control is delegated to the managers or governors.** – See S. 24 (1). The articles of government for a controlled secondary school are made by the Secretary of State, who thereby determines, among other things (see Chapter II, §3) what measure of the control exercised by the L.E.A. over the appointment of teachers shall be delegated to the governors. The articles, for example, may require the L.E.A. to appoint the head teacher on the recommendation of a joint committee consisting of an equal number of representatives of the L.E.A. and of the governors. The articles may also require that the assistant teachers in a controlled secondary school shall be appointed by the governors, subject, possibly, to the right of the L.E.A. to fill a vacancy by transferring a teacher from another school in their area, or from a group of new entrants to the teaching profession appointed by the L.E.A. to their service.

The rules of management for a controlled primary school are made by the L.E.A. and the L.E.A. may reserve to themselves the power of appointing the teachers, subject to the statutory powers of the managers concerning the head teacher (see note (*o*) below) and to the statutory powers of the foundation managers concerning reserved teachers (see note (*l*) below).

(*c*) **No teacher in a controlled school may be dismissed except by the authority.** – This condition is laid down in S.24 (1). For the conditions under which the foundation managers or foundation governors may require the L.E.A. to dismiss a reserved teacher see note (*m*) below. The articles of government of a controlled secondary school made by the Secretary of State may require the L.E.A. to consult the governors before dismissing a teacher and may provide that the governors shall be entitled to recommend the dismissal of a teacher. The rules of management for a controlled primary school are made by the L.E.A., and they may reserve to themselves the right to deal directly with the dismissal of teachers, subject to the statutory powers of the foundation managers concerning reserved teachers. It should be noted that here, as elsewhere, the education committee, or a sub-committee thereof, if the power has been delegated by the L.E.A., may act for the authority and deal with the dismissal of teachers.

(*d*) **Reserved Teacher.** – See S.27 (2).

(*e*) **Under the arrangements made by the foundation managers or foundation governors.** – See S.27 (1). The arrangements are to be made if the parents of any pupils attending the school make the request – see Chapter II, §4 – unless, owing to special circumstances, the foundation managers or foundation governors think it would be unreasonable to do so. See also Chapter II, §4, note (*j*).

(*f*) **And who is specifically appointed to give such instruction.** – See S.27 (2). The trust deed or previous practice may require denominational or undenominational instruction according to the particular circumstances of the school. In some secondary schools, for example, the trust deed requires that religious instruction shall be given in accordance with the Christian faith and the regulations made thereunder by the governors have provided for undenominational instruction. The minute of appointment or contract of service should specifically state that the teacher is appointed as a reserved teacher, and may particularize the requirement to be fulfilled or the undertaking to be given by the teacher. A reserved teacher may also give agreed syllabus instruction if he is prepared to do so.

(*g*) **Number of the teaching staff.** – See S. 27 (2). The number of the teaching staff means the establishment of teachers fixed by the L.E.A. for the school. A casual vacancy on the staff will not be deemed to reduce the number of the teaching staff.

Where the school consists of two or more departments, the number of teaching staff and of reserved teachers must be calculated by reference to the whole school.

(*h*) **No reserved teacher may be appointed on the staff of that school.** – See S. 27 (2). A controlled school with a total staff of one teacher or two teachers cannot have a reserved teacher. The foundation managers or foundation governors are not thereby exempted from their obligation under S.27 (1) to provide the special religious instruction for the pupils of parents who request them to do so. This point is made clear in the opening words of S.27 (2). In such circumstances, therefore, it will be open to the foundation managers or foundation governors to arrange for the instruction to be given by a clergyman, minister or by the head teacher or a non-reserved assistant teacher, if they are willing to do so – see Chapter II, §4, note (*j*). If the foundation managers or foundation governors can reasonably plead that they are unable to make such arrangements the provisions of S.27 (1) would exempt them from the necessity of doing so at the particular time. – See also Chapter II, §4, note (*l*). As to the unreasonable exercise of functions of managers and governors, see S.68.

(*i*) **Reserved teachers must be appointed on the staff.** – The duty is laid down in S.27 (2), and both the L.E.A. and the foundation managers or foundation governors have obligations to see that the duty is fulfilled.

(*j*) **The authority must consult the foundation managers or foundation governors,** by virtue of S.27 (4). The articles of government of a controlled secondary school may provide for the appointment of a reserved teacher by the governors after the foundation governors have expressed themselves satisfied that the person is fit and competent to give the required religious instruction. The L.E.A. before confirming the appointment, should satisfy themselves that the foundation governors have been consulted and have not declared themselves dissatisfied with the proposed appointment.

If, in the case of a controlled primary school, the L.E.A. directly appoint the teachers, they must consult the foundation managers before making the appointment of a reserved teacher for that school.

(*k*) **Required religious instruction.** – See Chapter II, §4, note (*i*).

(*l*) **The authority must not appoint that person as a reserved teacher in that school.** – See S. 27 (4). The foundation managers or foundation governors can veto the proposed appointment of a reserved teacher on the grounds mentioned; the L.E.A. may, therefor, give the foundation managers or foundation governors an opportunity of interviewing a teacher who is to be considered for appointment as a reserved teacher at the school. If the managers or governors veto a person as a reserved teacher that does not preclude the appointment of that person as a non-reserved teacher in that school or as a reserved teacher in another school.

(*m*) **May require the authority to dismiss him as a reserved teacher in that school.** – See S.27 (5). The reason must be nothing more and nothing less than that stated in the Act. – See *Smith v. Macnally* ([1912] 1 Ch. 816), in which the managers dismissed a teacher for alleged dissatisfaction with the religious instruction given by her, whereas the real ground was that she had ceased to be a member of the Church of England and had become a Wesleyan.

(*n*) **Must not while holding that position.** – See S.27 (3). Part of the religious agreement embodied in the Education Act, 1944, was that headships should be open, on equal terms, to all qualified teachers, whether reserved or non-reserved teachers. A teacher who has been a reserved teacher in another post, and who is appointed to the headship of a controlled school, must be so appointed as a non-reserved teacher. The head teacher, if willing to do so, may give trust deed (or previous practice) religious instruction under the arrangements made by the foundation managers or foundation governors, but it is entirely at the discretion of the head teacher, and must have nothing to do with his appointment or his holding office.

(*o*) **Must consider any representations made by the managers or governors.** – See S.27 (3). This is the statutory minimum part the managers or governors must have in the appointment of the head teacher.

In the case of a secondary school, the articles of government, made by the Minister, will normally require that the head teacher be appointed on the recommendation of a joint committee of the L.E.A. and governors. In the case of a primary school, the rules of management, made by the L.E.A., may provide for a joint committee of the primary education subcommittee of the L.E.A. and the managers to interview candidates and recommend the person for appointment as head teacher.

(*p*) **General conditions relating to non-reserved teachers.** – These conditions, popularly described as the 'teachers' charter', are laid down in S.30. They are to be observed by the L.E.A. and the managers or governors.

(*q*) **Or of his attending or omitting to attend religious worship,** *i.e.* in the school or elsewhere.

(*r*) **No such teacher,** *i.e.* a teacher who is not a reserved teacher.

(*s*) **No such teacher shall be required to give religious instruction.** – By S. 25 (2) the L.E.A. are under a statutory obligation to ensure that religious instruction is given in the school, but the Act gives the individual teacher the freedom to decide for himself, without consequential financial or professional disadvantage, whether he will give religious instruction. It follows that, in practice, a teacher who is to be considered for appointment as a non-reserved teacher should not be asked whether he is prepared to give religious instruction; and that a non-reserved teacher who is not prepared or able to give agreed syllabus religious instruction should not take up a post – *e.g.* the headship of a one-teacher school – if, by doing so the L.E.A. would be precluded from fulfilling their statutory obligation – to provide agreed syllabus religious instruction in the school – by means of the normal establishment of staff for that school.

A non-reserved teacher, if willing to do so, may give trust deed (or previous practice) religious instruction under the arrangements made by the foundation managers or foundation governors, but it is entirely at the discretion of the teacher, and must have nothing to do with his appointment or his holding office.

(*t*) **General conditions relating to reserved teachers.** – See the proviso to S.30. The reserved teacher has undertaken to give 'trust deed' religious instruction and has been appointed partly because of his fitness and competence to do so. The proviso to S.30 makes it clear that the reserved teacher is not to be placed at any financial or professional disadvantage because of the obligations he has undertaken.

(*u*) **By reason of marriage.** – See S. 24 (3).

# 7. *Other Employees at a Controlled School*

Any other persons (*a*) employed for the purposes of a controlled school are appointed and dismissed by the authority (*b*). The authority also determine their conditions of service. No person is to be disqualified for such employment (*c*) by reason of his religious opinion, or of his attending or omitting to attend religious worship.

## NOTES

(*a*) **Any other persons,** e.g. caretakers, cleaners, groundsmen – see S.22 (4); clerks to governors, correspondents, clerical staff, school meals staff.

(*b*) **Appointed and dismissed by the authority.** – That is to say they are to be appointed to the service of the authority and the authority may dismiss them. The articles of government or rules of management may provide for the delegation of the power of appointment and dismissal to the governors or managers, or of recommending appointment and dismissal to the authority. It is, however, the practice of the Secretary of State, in regard to the appointment of the correspondent to the managers of a controlled school, to deal with that in the instrument of management, which is made by the Secretary of State, and to provide that the appointment shall be made either by the managers or on their recommendation. In the case of articles of government for a controlled school, which are made by the Secretary of State, a corresponding provision is made regarding the appointment of the clerk to the governors. As regards school meals staff, the *Provisions of Milk and Meals Regulations, 1945*, require their appointment to the service of the L.E.A.

The official expenses of clerks to governors and correspondents, in connection with the maintenance of the school, and their salaries, are payable by the L.E.A., by virtue of S.114 (2) (*a*). These expenses are official postages, telephone calls, travelling expenses etc., in connection with the business of the L.E.A. and the managers or governors. The salary of the clerk to the governors or correspondent to the managers is determinable by the L.E.A. It is possible for a governor or a manager to be the clerk to the governors or the correspondent to the managers, respectively, but only if he receives no salary for the post, and acts in an honorary capacity.

The remuneration of a clerk to the governors or a correspondent to the managers, in respect of duties (such as the administration of any foundation income) not connected with the maintenance of the school by the L.E.A., is a matter for the governors or managers, or the foundation governors or foundation managers, as the case may be. The L.E.A. cannot reimburse them for any such expenditure.

(c) **For such employment.** – Disqualification on religious grounds, for any of the employments referred to in note (a) above, is prohibited by S.30.

# 8. *Maintenance and Use of Controlled School Premises*

From the date on which a school becomes a controlled school, the whole of the cost of maintaining the school premises will be assumed by the local education authority (a). The managers or governors will be responsible for any expenditure incurred in respect of the use of the school premises by them (b), or by persons to whom they may let them, out of school hours, such as the cost of heating and lighting, and any additional payment to the caretaker over and above his wage, paid by the authority, for extra duties performed by him for the managers or governors when the premises are so used. They are also responsible for certain insurances (see Chapter VII).

The foundation managers or foundation governors are entitled to determine the use to which the school premises or any part thereof shall be put on Sundays (c).

The managers or governors are entitled to determine the use to which the school premises or any part thereof shall by put on Saturdays (d), except when they are required for the purposes of the school, or by the authority for any educational purpose, including youth activities.

At all other times, the authority are entitled to give directions as they think fit (e) concerning the occupation and use of the school premises.

Any sum received by the managers, governors, or trustees, of the school, in respect of the letting or hiring of any part of the school premises, other than school buildings, must be paid to the authority (f). Any sum received by them for the letting or hiring of the school buildings will not be payable to the authority (g).

Under the Rating and Valuation Act, 1961, the premises of a controlled school are subject to the payment of rates by the authority, not by the managers or governors (h).

## NOTES

(a) **Will be assumed by the local education authority,** by virtue of S.15 (3) and the definition of maintenance contained in S.114 (2) (a). See also Chapter VII, §5 and §6.

(b) **In respect of the use of the school premises by them.** – All these items of expenditure on the use of the school premises by the managers or governors, or by persons to whom they may let the premises, are not expenditure on the maintenance of the school, as defined in S.114 (2) (a), and, therefore, the L.E.A. are neither responsible for the expenditure, nor have they the power to meet it.

(c) **The use to which the school premises shall be put on Sundays.** – See S.22 (1). The foundation managers or foundation governors exclusively determine such use.

(d) **The use to which the school premises shall be put on Saturdays.** – See S.22 (1). The managers or governors as a whole determine such use. The school premises consist of the school buildings, other buildings, and playing fields (see Chapter I, §2). First claim to the use of the whole or any part of the premises on Saturdays is

C cvs

reserved by the Act for the School, *i.e.* for a school session, or a school function, and for any educational use by the L.E.A. If only part of the premises is to be so used, the managers or governors can determine the use of the rest of the premises. If no part of the premises is to be so used on any Saturday, the managers or governors have the right to determine the use of the whole of the premises. Although the other buildings are part of the premises, the equipment in a school kitchen, etc., is the property of the L.E.A., and its use, if any, out of school hours, is under the control of the L.E.A. at all times.

(*e*) **Give directions as they think fit.** – By virtue of S.22 (1), the L.E.A. have the control of the use of the premises on weekdays for the exercise of their functions. If, out of school hours, the L.E.A. do not require the premises for that purpose, they cannot use S.22 (1) to stand in the way of the reasonable use of the premises by the managers, governors, or trustees, or of the letting by them for other reasonable use.

(*f*) **Must be paid to the authority.** – By virtue of *S.4 (1)*. The income from lettings which must be paid to the L.E.A. are those in respect of the other buildings (see Chapter I, §2). The rent for the caretaker's house on the site, if any, must be paid to the L.E.A., who are responsible for the whole of its maintenance, as it is part of the school premises. Income from lettings of the school meals kitchen, if allowed by the L.E.A., and of the room, if any, that has been exclusively set apart by the L.E.A. for school dining, and from the use of the playing fields provided by the L.E.A., again if allowed by the L.E.A., must be paid to the L.E.A.

(*g*) **Will not be payable to the authority.** – Any income from lettings of the school buildings (see Chapter I, §2) is not payable to the L.E.A. If there are school trustees, the income will normally be payable to them. In that event, the local arrangement will presumably provide that any expenditure payable to the L.E.A. for such use for heating, lighting, etc., will be met by the trustees, though the L.E.A. will look to the managers or governors for their money. Similarly, in the case of a privately-owned school, if the income from lettings is payable to the owner.

(*h*) **Premises of a controlled school are subject to the payment of rates.** – S.64 of the Education Act, 1944, exempted all maintained voluntary schools from rates, an exemption previously given to non-provided public elementary schools. S.29 of the Rating and Valuation Act, 1961, however, repealed S.64 of the Education Act, 1944, and provided for the payment of rates on maintained voluntary schools. On maintained voluntary schools opened before April 1st, 1963, no rates were payable in the financial year 1963–64, in 1964–65 one-fifth of the amount otherwise due, two-fifths in 1965–66, and so on, full payment to begin in 1968–69. No such abatement applies for schools opened on or after April 1st, 1963. S.12 of the same Act made the payment of rates on maintained voluntary schools an item of maintenance under S.114 (2) (*a*) of the Education Act, 1944, *i.e.* made the rates payable by the L.E.A., not by the managers or governors.

S.11 of the Rating and Valuation Act, 1961, gave the right of mandatory relief of 50 per cent of the rates otherwise chargeable for 'any hereditament occupied by, or by trustees for, a charity and wholly or mainly used for charitable purposes', and allowed the local rating authority to go further, if they wished, and give 100 per cent relief of rates on such hereditaments.

The goverment held that such hereditaments included maintained voluntary schools of every kind – aided, special agreement, and controlled. Local authority associations, including the County Councils Association, take the view that in the case of a controlled school, it is the L.E.A. who are the paramount occupiers of the school premises, and therefore that the reliefs of S.11 just mentioned are not available to controlled schools. That point has not, so far, been tested in the Courts, mainly because the same local authority associations consider that as it is the L.E.A., not the managers or governors of a voluntary school, who have to pay the rates, there is some doubt about the 50 per cent mandatory relief, and the 100 per cent discretionary relief, for any kind of maintained voluntary school, and consider that the Minister of Housing and Local Government should so order, as he has power to do, by including maintained voluntary schools in the First Schedule of the Rating and Valuation Act, 1961.

It should be noted that although the 50 per cent mandatory relief, or the discretionary 100 per cent relief, goes to the L.E.A. from the local rating authority, a claim for such reliefs has to be made to the local rating authority by the managers or governors of the maintained voluntary school. Many did so at the request of their L.E.A. made soon after the Act came into force. But many local rating authorities, although accepting a payment on account for rates on maintained schools, where claims were made for the 50 per cent mandatory relief, have not admitted their obligation to give such relief, during the continuance of the dispute mentioned. And in the absence of any change of opinion by the government, some L.E.A.s are making arrangements with the local rating authorities so that the latter do not give the L.E.A. the relief mentioned.

# III. THE AIDED SCHOOL

## 1. *Capital Expenditure on School Premises*

Capital expenditure on the premises of an aided school may be involved in one of the four following ways: **1** the alteration of the premises of an existing school; **2** the transfer of an existing school to a new site; **3** the substitution of a new school for one or more existing voluntary schools; **4** the establishment of a new school.

The provisions of the Education Acts for each of these cases are given below:

### (1) Alteration of an Existing Aided School

The managers or governors are responsible for the capital expenditure on the following alterations (*a*) to the premises (*b*) of an existing aided school: the improvement or enlargement (*c*) of, or additions to, the school buildings (*d*). Towards this expenditure the Secretary of State will make a maintenance contribution of 80 per cent (*e*). Any other capital expenditure on the school premises, such as an addition to the existing site (*f*), the improvement of the school grounds (*g*), frontagers' road charges, the alteration or provision of other buildings (*h*), or the provision or extension of playing fields and boundary walls or fence to such fields (*i*), is to be met by the local education authority.

The authority must convey their interest in any addition to the site, and in any buildings thereon which are to form part of the school premises, to the trustees of the school (*j*); but the legitimate interests of the authority and of the Secretary of State are protected in the event of the discontinuance of the school by the managers or governors (*k*), and if part or the whole of the premises are acquired from the trustees by any person (*l*).

Any playing fields provided by the authority and any buildings on them provided by the authority, for use in connection therewith, remain the property of the authority (*m*). The authority may carry out this work (*n*).

The expenses of discharging any liability (*o*) incurred by the managers or governors, or on their behalf, or by or on behalf of any former managers or governors or trustees, in connection with the provision of the premises or equipment for the purposes of the school, before April 1st, 1945, are to be met by the managers or governors; any such expenditure will not be eligible for a maintenance contribution from the Secretary of State (*p*). But in special circumstances in the case of an aided secondary school the authority may continue to meet or to assist the governors to meet such liabilities (*q*) and any deficit on their previous maintenance account (*r*).

### (2) Transfer of an Existing Aided School to a New Site and Disposal of Old School Premises

If an existing aided school has to be transferred to a new site (*s*) the local education authority must meet the cost of the new site (*t*) and the cost of the school grounds, any road charges, and any other buildings (*u*) required for the purposes of the school. The authority must also convey their interest in the site and other buildings on it to the trustees of the school ($v$); but the legitimate interests of the authority and of the Secretary of State are protected in the event of the discontinuance of the school by the managers or governors ($w$), and if part or the whole of the premises are acquired from the trustees by any person ($x$).

The authority must also provide the playing fields ($y$), boundary walls or fence to such fields, and any buildings on them required for use in connection therewith. The authority may carry out this work ($z$), and the playing fields and any buildings on them, provided by the authority for use in connection therewith, remain the property of the authority.

The managers or governors must provide the new school buildings ($a^1$); but, after taking into account any sums which may accrue to the managers, governors or trustees of the school in respect of the disposal of the site of the existing premises ($b^1$), the Secretary of State will make to the managers or governors a grant of 80 per cent of the cost of their approved expenditure in providing the new school buildings.

Any continuing liabilities ($c^1$) of the managers or governors, their predecessors or trustees, on the existing premises and equipment for the purposes of the school are to be met by them, and any such expenditure will not be eligible for a maintenance contribution from the Secretary of State ($d^1$). But in special circumstances in the case of an aided secondary school, the authority may assist the governors ($e^1$) to meet such liabilities and any deficit on their previous maintenance account ($f^1$).

### (3) Substitution of a New Aided School for one or more Existing Voluntary Schools

If a new aided school is established in substitution for one or more existing voluntary schools ($g^1$), the new site, the new school grounds, any road charges in respect of the site, and the new school buildings ($h^1$) must be provided by the managers or governors; but, after taking into account any sums which may accrue to the managers, governors or trustees of the school from the disposal of the site or sites of the voluntary schools which are discontinued ($i^1$), the Secretary of State will pay to the managers or governors a grant of 80 per cent of their approved expenditure in providing the new site and the new school buildings, including the school grounds and any road charges in respect of the site.

The local education authority must provide the other buildings on the site required for the new aided school ($j^1$), which, being built on the site owned by the trustees of the school, become their property. The legitimate interests of the authority and of the Secretary of State are protected in the event of the discontinuance of the school by the managers or governors ($k^1$).

The authority must also provide the playing fields ($l^1$), boundary walls or fence to such fields, and any buildings on them required for use in connection therewith. The authority may carry out this work ($m^1$), and such playing fields and such buildings remain the property of the authority ($n^1$).

Any continuing liabilities ($o^1$) of the managers or governors, their predecessors or trustees, in respect of the premises and equipment of the discontinued school or schools must be met by the managers or governors, and any such expenditure will not be eligible for a maintenance contribution from the Secretary of State ($p^1$). But in special circumstances in the case of an aided secondary school, the authority may meet or assist the governors to meet such liabilities and any deficit on their previous maintenance account ($q^1$).

### (4) Establishment of a New Aided School

If a new aided school is established ($r^1$), the new site, the new school grounds, and the new school buildings ($s^1$), must be provided by the managers or governors, who are also responsible for any road charges in respect of the site. The Secretary of State will pay to the managers or governors a grant of 80 per cent of their approved expenditure on that provision.

Similarly, if the school premises of an aided school are altered to such an extent as to amount to the establishment of a new school ($t^1$), any alterations or additions to the site, to the school grounds, and to the school buildings, required for that purpose, together with any road charges in respect of the site, thereby involved, must be paid for by the managers or governors, who will receive a grant of 80 per cent of their approved expenditure thereon from the Secretary of State.

The local education authority must provide the other buildings ($u^1$) on the site required for the new aided school, which, being built on the site belonging to the school trustees, become their property. The legitimate interests of the authority and of the Secretary of State are protected in the event of the discontinuance of the school by the managers or governors ($v^1$).

The authority must also provide the playing fields ($w^1$), the boundary walls or fence to such fields, and any buildings on them required for use in connection therewith. The authority may carry out this work ($x^1$), and the playing fields and any buildings on them provided by the authority for use in connection therewith, remain the property of the authority ($y^1$).

### NOTES

(*a*) **Alterations** are defined in S.114 (1)* as improvements, enlargements or additions to the school premises which do not amount to the establishment of a new school (see S.67 (4)). In so far as these are alterations to the school buildings (see Chapter I, §2), the expenditure on them is the responsibility of the managers or governors, by S.15 (3)*.

(*b*) **Premises.** – For definition of school premises see Chapter I, §2.

(*c*) **Enlargement,** that is an enlargement that does not amount to the establishment of a new school – see S.114 (1)*.

(*d*) **School buildings.** – See Chapter I, §2.

(*e*) **Maintenance contribution of 80 per cent.** – By S.102 as amended by S.1 (1) of the Education Act, 1967, the maintenance contribution payable by the Secretary of State is 80 per cent.

(*f*) **Addition to the existing site.** – The duty of the L.E.A. to provide is set out in *S.3 and §1 of the First Schedule*. Any expenditure on this addition to the site to make it suitable for building purposes must, by *§3 of the First Schedule*, be borne by the L.E.A. If such an addition to the site has any buildings on it that are of value for the purposes of the school buildings, that value will be debited to the managers or governors (see *§4 of the First Schedule*), since it is their duty to provide school buildings.

(g) **Improvement of the school grounds** – *e.g.* improvement, or provision, of playground, boundary walls or fences to the site, roads and paths on the site, is an obligation to be met by the L.E.A., as it is excluded from the duty of the managers or governors by S.15 (3)*, and is, therefore, by S.114 (2) (*a*), included in the duty of the L.E.A. to maintain the school. For definition of school grounds, see Chapter I, §2.

(h) **Other buildings.** – See Chapter I, §2, *i.e.* buildings which, by virtue of *S.4*, are not school buildings. The alteration of these other buildings is not included in the duties of the managers or governors under S.15 (3)*, and is, therefore, included in the duty of the L.E.A. under S.114 (2) (*a*) to maintain the school. Nevertheless, although a caretaker's dwelling is an 'other building' (see Chapter I, §2) and not a school building, the L.E.A. are under no obligation to provide a caretaker's house at an aided school, and they may prefer not to do so, but to leave it to the managers or governors to provide, if they wish to do so, on their own land, as the caretaker is their employee, not the employee of the L.E.A. If the L.E.A. do build a caretaker's house on the school site, the rent is to be paid over to them, by the provisions of *S.4* (*I*), and the L.E.A. will be responsible for the maintenance of the house.

(i) **Playing fields.** – See Chapter II, §1, note (*e*), which also applies to an aided school.

(j) **Trustees of the school.** – See Chapter II, §1, note (*i*). The provisions of the Act, referred to in that note, apply to the case of an altered aided school.

(k) **Discontinuance of the school by the managers or governors.** – See Chapter II, §1, note (*j*). Similar provisions apply to the case of an altered aided school.

(l) **If part or the whole of the premises are acquired from the trustees by any person.** – See Chapter II, §1, note (*k*). Similar provisions apply to the case of an altered aided school.

(m) **Playing fields remain the property of the authority.** – See Chapter II, §1, note (*m*). The same provisions apply to the case of an altered aided school.

(n) **Authority may carry out this work,** because the provision of playing fields and buildings thereon is a duty of the L.E.A., who are the owners of such part of the premises. The L.E.A. also have power to carry out alterations in respect of their requirements for the school meals service (see *Provision of Milk and Meals Regulations, 1945*) and the articles of government and rules of management may give the L.E.A. power to carry out alterations to the school buildings, other buildings, and site, in the case of expenditure for which they are responsible. See also Chapter III, §8, notes (*c*) and (*d*).

(o) **Discharging any liability.** – By virtue of S.15 (3)*, these are the responsibility of the managers or governors; but see notes (*q*) and (*r*) below.

(p) **Not be eligible for a mantenance contribution from the Secretary of State.** – Expenses in discharging any of these liabilities incurred before April 1st, 1945, are not included in S.102 in the items of expenditure towards which the Secretary of State is to pay a maintenance contribution.

(q) **Authority may meet or assist the governors to meet such liabilities.** – By virtue of S.66. It is important to note, however, that this provision of the Education Act, 1944, is intended to apply only to a strictly limited set of special circumstances, namely, those in which, under the Education Act, 1921, the L.E.A. had met or were meeting certain expenditure on grammar schools assisted by them. This provision was added to the Education Bill at the Report stage in the House of Commons, with the following explanation given by the Minister (see *Hansard*, May 9th, 1944, cols 1855–56): 'This is an amendment to enable a local education authority, if they think fit and the Minister approves, to assist the governors of a secondary school of grammar school type to meet liabilities incurred before the date of the commencement of Part II of the Act. The amendment is strictly limited in character, and required for a strictly limited purpose to carry on existing practice – for example, to enable the authority to continue to help – I underline those words – to pay off loans, to meet expenditure on the school premises where the authority had previously given that assistance by way of a deficiency grant under the existing law.'

(r) **Any deficit on their previous maintenance account.** – In S.66 the phrase, 'for the purpose of establishing and carrying on the school' is wider than the phrase 'in connection with the provision of premises or equipment for the purposes of the school', which, by the Education Act, 1946, has been substituted for the former phrase in S.15 (3) (*a*)*, but not in S.66. Hence, with the Minister's approval, the L.E.A. were empowered to meet or to assist the governors to meet the deficit on the maintenance account of an aided secondary school as at March 31st, 1945, and can, in the special circumstances referred to in note (*q*) above, meet or assist the governors to meet their continuing liabilities in respect of the provision of the existing premises or the existing equipment for the purposes of the school.

(*s*) **Transferred to a new site.** – See Chapter II, §1, note (*n*). The same conditions apply to the transfer of an existing aided school to a new site. The transfer of a school to a new site is ordered by the Secretary of State because it is not possible to alter the premises on the existing site to the standards of the 1944 Act. Because of that, the Act apportions the expenditure of transfer between the managers or governors, the L.E.A., and the Secretary of State, in the same way as in the case of an alteration of a school on its existing site, or on an addition to that site.

(*t*) **Cost of the new site.** – The duty of the L.E.A. to meet this cost is contained in *S.3* and *§1 of the First Schedule.*

(*u*) **The school grounds and any other buildings.** – The duty of the managers or governors is restricted to the provision of the new school buildings by *S.3 and §2 of the First Schedule.* The duty of the L.E.A. to provide the school grounds and the other buildings is included in their duty to maintain the school under S.114 (2) (*a*), coupled with *S.3 and §2 of the First Schedule.* For definition of 'school grounds' and 'other buildings', see Chapter I, §2. See also note (*h*) above.

(*v*) **Trustees of the school.** – See note (*r*) of Chapter II, §1, which, so far as it refers to the appointment of trustees, and the conveyance of the new site to them, equally applies to the case of a transferred aided school.

(*w*) **Discontinuance of the school by the managers or governors.** – The legitimate interests of the L.E.A. and of the Secretary of State, in respect of capital expenditure incurred by them on the premises, are protected by S.14 (1)* in the event of the discontinuance of the school by the managers or governors.

(*x*) **If part or the whole of the premises are acquired from the trustees by any person.** – See Chapter II, §1, note (*k*). The same provisions apply to the case of a transferred aided school in respect of that part of the capital expenditure met by the L.E.A.

(*y*) **Playing fields.** – See Chapter II, §1, note (*e*). The same provisions apply to the case of a transferred aided school.

(*z*) **Authority may carry out this work,** because the provision of playing fields and buildings thereon for use in connection therewith is a duty of the L.E.A., who are the owners of such part of the premises.

($a^1$) **New school buildings.** – See note (*u*) above. S.8 (1) of the Education (Miscellaneous Provisions) Act, 1953, amends S.103 (1), with respect to the payment of grant by the Secretary of State to the managers or governors, in such a way as to make it clear that the grant is payable towards the purchase or towards the purchase and adaptation of an existing building to which the school may be transferred in exactly the same way as if brand new school buildings are provided for the transferred school. By S.103 (1) as amended by S.1 (1) of the Education Act, 1967, the rate of the Secretary of State's grant is 80 per cent.

($b^1$) **Disposal of the site of the existing premises.** – The disposal of the site of the existing premises includes the disposal of any school buildings and any other buildings on it, except a teacher's house which is excluded from the definition of school premises (see Chapter I, §2).

The sums from this disposal must be taken into account by the Secretary of State, by virtue of S.103 (3), in determining the amount of grant made by him to the managers or governors in respect of the new school buildings. In some cases, the old site may be so valuable that the managers, governors or trustees may receive more for its disposal than the cost to them of providing the new school buildings. In such cases the Secretary of State will make no grant. But in the normal case in which the provision of the new school buildings costs the managers, governors or trustees, more than they receive for the disposal of the old site, the Secretary of State will make his grant, at the rate mentioned in note ($a^1$) above, towards the difference. If the managers, governors, or trustees, receive nothing for the old site, *e.g.* because the trust permits it to be used for some other purpose, when it ceases to be used for the school and is so used, nothing will be deducted by the Secretary of State in determining his grant towards the new school buildings.

It should be noticed that any playing fields of the old school premises are not included in the disposal of the old site for the above-mentioned calculation of grant, because playing fields, by virtue of *S.16 (1)*, are excluded from the definition of site. Such playing fields remain the property of the owners. It may, of course, be practicable to use them in connection with the new school premises.

(*c*) **Continuing liabilities.** – These are to be met by the managers or governors by virtue of S.15 (3)\*; but see notes (*q*) and (*r*) above.

(*d*[1]) **Not be eligible for a maintenance contribution from the Secretary of State.** – See note (*p*) above.

(*e*[1]) **Authority may assist the governors.** – See note (*q*) above.

(*f*[1]) **Any deficit on their previous maintenance accounts.** – See note (*r*) above.

(*g*[1]) **Substitution for one or more existing voluntary schools.** – The conditions under which a new aided school may be substituted for one or more existing voluntary schools are set out in S.16 (2). Substitution does not arise if a voluntary school is merely transferred to a new site in order that the premises may conform to the standards prescribed under the Education Act, 1944. Substitution for one existing voluntary school arises if the new provision is to be greater than that required for the pupils from the voluntary school to be discontinued. Substitution for two or more existing voluntary schools arises if the new provision is to be equal to or greater than that required for the pupils from the voluntary schools to be discontinued. It is not possible to use the procedure of substitution for the replacement of parts of voluntary schools: substitution involves the discontinuance of whole schools. On the other hand, if an existing voluntary school consisting of two separate departments is first converted into two separate schools by the procedure laid down by *S.2*, either of the separate schools can then take part in a substitution process. On substitution, discontinuance of a school replaced is automatic, and the provisions of S.14 do not apply.

(*h*[1]) **New site and the new school buildings.** – As the new school is an aided school, the provisions of S.13 (2) and S.13 (7)\*, coupled with *S.3 and sub-paragraph (a) of the proviso to §1 of the First Schedule*, require the managers or governors to provide the new site, including the school grounds, and the new school buildings. Under S.1 (2) of the Education Act, 1967, grant will be paid by the Secretary of State towards the expenditure of the managers or governors on all those items, and will not be limited, as was previously the case, to the proportion of those items in the new provision that would have sufficed to provide equivalent accommodation for the pupils from the discontinued schools. Again, by S.1 (2) of the Education Act, 1967, the same grant arrangements will apply where the managers or governors buy a property and adapt it for the purpose of the substituted school.

(*i*[1]) **Disposal of the site or sites of the voluntary schools which are discontinued.** – Under S.103 (3), the Secretary of State, in determining the amount of his grant to the managers or governors of a substituted aided school, was required to take into account any sums which might accrue to the managers, governors, or trustees of the school in respect of the disposal of the sites of the discontinued schools. That requirement remains under the Education Act, 1967, even though that Act has removed all references to substituted schools in S.103. The requirement is continued by virtue of S.1 (3) of the Education Act, 1967, that being the sole purpose of that subsection, as the Secretary of State said on the second reading of the Bill. The disposal of the site of a discontinued school includes any school and other buildings on it, except a teacher's house which is excluded from the definition of school premises (see Chapter I, §2). Playing fields of discontinued schools are not included in the disposal of the old sites, because, by *S.16 (1)*, they are excluded from the definition of site. Such playing fields remain the property of the owners. It may, of course, be practicable to use them in connection with the substituted school.

In some cases, the site or sites of the discontinued school or schools may be so valuable that the managers, governors, or trustees of the substituted school may receive more from their disposal than the cost to them of the new substituted school. In such cases they will receive no grant from the Secretary of State. But in the normal case in which the expenditure of the managers or governors in providing the substituted school is greater than the amount which they or the trustees receive from the disposal of the old site or sites, the Secretary of State will make his grant, at the rate of 80 per cent, towards the difference. If the managers, governors, or trustees, receive nothing for the old sites, *e.g.* because the trusts of the discontinued schools permit them to be used for some other purpose when they cease to be used as schools, and they are so used, nothing will be deducted by the Secretary of State in determining the amount of his grant towards the substituted school. The rate of grant of 80 per cent towards a substituted school is laid down by S.1 (2) of the Education Act, 1967.

($j^1$) **Other buildings required for the new aided school.** – In the case of a new aided school, the duty of the L.E.A. to provide the other buildings is laid down in S.13 (7)\*. There is no obligation on the L.E.A. to provide a caretaker's house, and they may prefer to leave that provision to the managers or governors. – See note (*h*) above.

($k^1$) **Discontinuance of the school by the managers or governors.** – See Chapter II, §1, note (*j*). The same provisions apply to the case of a new substituted aided school in respect of the capital expenditure incurred by the L.E.A. and in respect of the capital grants made by the Secretary of State.

($l^1$) **Playing fields.** – In the case of a new aided school, the duty of the L.E.A. to provide the playing fields and any buildings on them required for use in connection therewith is laid down in S.13 (7)\*.

($m^1$) **Authority may carry out this work.** – See note (*z*) above.

($n^1$) **Playing fields remain the property of the authority.** – See Chapter II, §1, note (*m*). The same provisions apply to the case of a new aided school.

($o^1$) **Continuing liabilities.** – See note (*o*) above.

($p^1$) **Not be eligible for a maintenance contribution from the Secretary of State.** – See note (*p*) above.

($q^1$) **Any deficit on their previous maintenance account.** – See notes (*q*) and (*r*) above.

($r^1$) **If a new aided school is established.** – The establishment of any new school to be maintained by a L.E.A. requires the approval of the Secretary of State under S.13. By S.1 (2) of the Education Act, 1967, all new aided schools are now eligible for grant-aid by the Secretary of State towards their provision by the managers or governors. The previous limitation of such grant-aid to substituted schools, to schools to the extent to which they provided accommodation for displaced pupils, or to secondary schools provided to match the accommodation of certain primary schools, under the 1959 Act, are all removed. The term 'displaced pupil' disappears from the Education Acts, by S.1 (5) of the Education Act, 1967, and the limiting provisions of the Education Act, 1959, just mentioned, are also superseded by S.1 of the new Act.

Towards the approved expenditure of the managers or governors on the provision of a newly established aided school, described in §1 (4) of Chapter III, the Secretary of State will make a grant of 80 per cent. The corresponding provisions in the case of a new substituted aided school have been dealt with in §1 (3) of Chapter III.

($s^1$) **New site and new school buildings.** – As the new school is an aided school, the provisions of S.13 (2) and S.13 (7)\*, coupled with *S.3 and sub-paragraph (a) of the proviso to §1 of the First Schedule*, require the managers or governors to provide the new site, including the school grounds, and the new school buildings, and to pay for any road charges in respect of the site. S.1 (2) of the Education Act, 1967, also makes it clear that the same grant arrangements will apply where the managers or governors buy a property and adapt it for the purpose of establishing the new aided school.

($t^1$) **To such an extent as to amount to the establishment of a new school.** – The determination by the Secretary of State whether a proposed alteration amounts to the establishment of a new school is made under S.67 (4). If the alteration is to provide accommodation for an increase in the number of pupils of more than 25 per cent, the Secretary of State will regard it as amounting to the establishment of a new school. Paragraph (*b*) of S.1 (2) of the Education Act, 1967, refers to such cases, and makes it clear that the approved expenditure of the managers or governors on the alterations will be grant-aided at the rate of 80 per cent. The items in the alterations for which the managers or governors are responsible correspond, and for the same reasons, to those mentioned in note ($s^1$).

($u^1$) **Other buildings.** – See note ($j^1$) above.

($v^1$) **Discontinuance of the school by the managers or governors.** – See note ($k^1$) above.

($w^1$) **Playing fields.** – See note ($l^1$) above.

($x^1$) **Authority may carry out this work.** – See note (*z*) above.

($y^1$) **Remain the property of the authority.** – See Chapter II, §1, note (*m*). The same provisions apply to the case of a new aided school.

# 2. Instrument and Rules of Management of an Aided Primary School

The instrument of management (a) of an aided primary school, which provides for the constitution of the body of managers, is made by an order of the Secretary of State (b). Subject to a minimum of six managers, the number will be determined by the Secretary of State, after consultation with the local education authority (c). If there are six managers, they will be appointed as follows: four Foundation Managers (d), one L.E.A., one Minor Authority (e). If there are nine managers, as follows: six Foundation Managers, two L.E.A., one Minor Authority.

The rules of management (f) are made by an order of the authority. These rules govern the conduct of the school, subject to the provisions of the Education Acts (g) and of any trust deed of the school (h).

If the Secretary of State considers that anything included or proposed to be included in the instrument or rules of management is inconsistent with the trust deed, and if he thinks it just and expedient, in the interests of the school, that the trust deed should be modified (i) to remove the inconsistency, he may make an order modifying the trust deed (j). But before doing so, he is bound to give an opportunity to the authority, and to any other persons who appear to him to be concerned with the management of the school, to make representations to him; and he must also have regard to all the circumstances of the school, and, in the case of an existing school, to the manner in which it has previously been conducted.

Specimen instrument and rules of management for an aided primary school are given in the Appendix.

## NOTES

(a) **Instrument of management.** – See S.17 (1). The instrument besides fixing the constitution and method of appointment of the managers, in accordance with the provisions of the Education Acts, also regulates the proceedings of the managers in accordance with S.21 and the Fourth Schedule, as amended by the Education (Miscellaneous Provisions) Act, 1948. Special provision for the grouping of two or more schools under one managing body may be made with the consent of the voluntary school managers – see S.20. All matters coming within the purview of the managers of an aided school stand referred to the whole of the managers – see Note to §18 of Specimen Instrument given in the Appendix.

(b) **Order of the Secretary of State.** – See S.17 (2).

(c) **After consultation with the local education authority.** – See Chapter II, §2, note (c).

(d) **Foundation managers.** – See Chapter II, §2, note (d).

(e) **Minor authority.** – See Chapter II, §2, note (e).

(f) **Rules of management.** – See S.17 (3) (a).

(g) **Subject to the provisions of the Education Acts.** – By S.17 (3) the rules must be made by the L.E.A. But, with regard to the question of consent of the L.E.A. to the appointment of teachers it should be noted that S.24 (2) (b) provides that the rules 'may make such provision as may be agreed between the local education authority and the managers or governors of the school, or in default of such agreement as may be determined by the Secretary of State, for enabling the authority to prohibit the appointment, without the consent of the authority, of teachers to be employed for giving secular instruction, and for enabling the authority to give directions as to the educational qualifications of the teachers to be so employed'. In making the Rules of Management for an aided school the L.E.A. are not obliged to consult the managers on any other provisions of the rules.

(h) **And of any trust deed of the school.** – See Chapter II, §2, note (h).

(i) **That the trust deed should be modified.** – See Chapter II, §2, note (i).

(j) **Order modifying the trust deed.** – See Chapter II, §2, note (j).

## 3. Instrument and Articles of Government of an Aided Secondary School

The instrument of government (a) of an aided secondary school, which provides for the constitution of the body of governors, is made by an order of the Secretary of State (b). The number of governors will be determined by the Secretary of State after consultation with the local education authority, but two-thirds must be foundation governors (c) and one-third must be governors appointed by the authority (d).

The articles of government (e) are made by an order of the Secretary of State. These articles govern the conduct of the school, subject to the provisions of the Education Acts and of any trust deed of the school (f), and the articles must, in particular, define the functions to be exercised by the authority, the governors and the head teacher.

If the Secretary of State considers that anything included or proposed to be included in the instrument or articles of government is inconsistent with the trust deed, and if he thinks it is just and expedient, in the interests of the school, that the trust deed should be modified (g) to remove the inconsistency, he may make an order modifying the trust deed. But before doing so, he is bound to give an opportunity to the authority, and to any other persons who appear to him to be concerned with the government of the school, to make representations to him; and he must have regard to all the circumstances of the school, and, in the case of an existing school, to the manner in which it has previously been conducted.

Specimen instrument and articles of government for an aided secondary school are given in the Appendix.

### NOTES

(a) **Instrument of government.** – See S.17 (1). The instrument besides fixing the constitution and the method of appointment of the governors, in accordance with the provisions of the Education Acts, also regulates the proceedings of the governors in accordance with S.21 and the Fourth Schedule as amended by the Education (Miscellaneous Provisions) Act, 1948. Special provision may be made with the consent of the governors of voluntary schools for the grouping of two or more schools under one governing body – see S.20. All matters coming within the purview of the governors of an aided school stand referred to the whole of the governors – see note to §18 of specimen instrument given in the Appendix. In some aided secondary schools there may be a separate governing body established under a previous scheme for the administration of certain endowments.

(b) **Order of the Secretary of State.** – See S.17 (2).

(c) **Foundation governors.** – See Chapter II, §2, note (d). The same provisions also apply to foundation governors. See also S.19 (2) (b).

(d) **Governors appointed by the authority.** – See. S.19 (2) (b). The total number of governors, foundation and authority governors, must be a multiple of three.

(e) **Articles of government.** – See Chapter II, §3, note (e). See also S.24 (2) (b) referred to in note (g) to Chapter III, §2.

(f) **Trust deed of the school.** – See Chapter II, §3, note (f).

(g) **That the trust deed should be modified.** – See Chapter II, §3, note (g).

## 4. Religious Worship and Religious Instruction in an Aided School

The school day in an aided school must begin with collective worship (a) for all pupils, except those who have been withdrawn (b) from such worship by their parents. Except on any special occasion (*c*), the religious worship must take place on the school premises, and, unless the managers or governors consider that the premises make the arrangement impracticable, a single act of worship must be arranged (*d*).

The Education Acts do not specify the character of the religious worship (*e*) in an aided school, but it is under the control of the managers or governors, subject to any provisions of the trust deed relating to worship.

Religious instruction must be given in the school (*f*), but a parent may withdraw his pupil from such instruction (*g*), or may withdraw his pupil from the school in order to receive religious instruction, of a kind which is not provided in the school, elsewhere. The religious instruction given in the school (*h*) must be in accordance with the trust deed relating to the school, or, where provision for that purpose is not made by such a deed, in accordance with the practice observed before the school became an aided school.

If, however, the parents of pupils desire them to receive agreed syllabus instruction (*i*), and if the pupils concerned cannot with reasonable convenience attend a school in which such instruction is available (*j*), then, unless the authority are satisfied that owing to any special circumstances it would be unreasonable to do so, arrangements must be made for agreed syllabus instruction for those pupils in the school during the times set apart for religious instruction (*k*). These arrangements must ordinarily be made by the managers or governors, but if the authority are satisfied that the managers or governors are unwilling to make the arrangements, the authority must make the arrangements themselves.

The conditions under which (*l*) a pupil may be withdrawn from the school by his parents in order to receive religious instruction, of a kind not provided in the school, elsewhere, are as follows: (i) the authority must be satisfied that the pupil cannot reasonably attend a school at which the desired religious instruction is given; (ii) the authority must be satisfied that arrangements have, in fact, been made for the pupil to receive the desired religious instruction elsewhere; (iii) the withdrawal of the pupil can only be made at the beginning or at the end of the school session, and only for such periods as are reasonably necessary.

A pupil must not be required (*m*), as a condition of attending the school, either to attend or to abstain from attending a Sunday School or a place of religious worship.

The religious instruction given in an aided school is to be under the control of the managers or governors (*n*). Except as regards any agreed syllabus instruction given in the school, the arrangements for the inspection of the religious instruction (*o*) are to be made by the managers or governors.

The inspection of any agreed syllabus instruction (*p*) given in an aided school may only be carried out by the following persons: (i) one of H.M. Inspectors, (ii) a person appointed by the Secretary of State as an additional inspector and ordinarily employed for the purpose of inspecting secular instruction, (iii) an officer in the full-time employment of the authority who is ordinarily employed for the purpose of inspecting secular instruction.

## NOTES

(*a*) **Must begin with collective worship,** by virtue of S.25 (1).

(*b*) **Except those who have been withdrawn.** – Chapter II, §4, note (*b*). The same provisions apply to an aided school. A parent's withdrawal of his pupil from religious worship also applies to the special occasions (see note (*c*) below) on which the religious worship is held elsewhere than on the school premises.

(*c*) **Except on any special occasion.** – By virtue of *S.*7 the religious worship in an aided school must normally take place on the school premises. *S.*7 (2) provides for the worship to take place elsewhere, *e.g.* in church, on any special occasion, if the managers or governors consider it desirable, but also lays down the rule that the worship must normally take place on the school premises. They must also see that the religious worship elsewhere on the special occasion only takes place at the beginning of the school day – see *S.*7 (2). Any such special occasions must be entered in the school record, and there must be a note on the time-table of the school stating where the worship takes place.

The Ministry of Education added, in Circular No. 111, that it is important that parents should be given adequate notice of any proposal to hold the collective act of worship off the school premises in case they should wish their pupils to be excused from attending; that the method of informing parents will be affected by local circumstances, but that it will not be sufficient only to make the time-table entry required by the statutory regulations; and that a notice of the special occasion should be prominently displayed in the school, if possible not less than fourteen days beforehand, and the pupils be instructed to inform their parents.

By S.39 (2) (*b*), there is no obligation on a parent to send his pupil to school on any day exclusively set apart for religious observance by the body to which the parent belongs; but this provision must not be interpreted to mean that the requirements of the Act as to the number of days on which a school is to meet in any educational year need not be fulfilled. The managers or governors may resolve that the school shall have an occasional holiday within the number of days allowed for such holidays on any particular day, *e.g.* Ascension Day. But the organization of a religious service for the pupils who absent themselves from school on such a day, or for any of the pupils if an occasional holiday is taken on that day, is an arrangement made by the church as the pupils are not then attending school.

(*d*) **A single act of worship must be arranged.** – See S.25 (1).

(*e*) **Character of the religious worship.** – If, as is sometimes the case, the character of the religious worship is not specified in the trust deed, the managers or governors will presumably maintain the practice formerly observed. If the managers or governors so decide, a clergyman or minister, according to the denomination of the school, may conduct the religious worship on any occasion. Such occasions should be entered in the school record.

(*f*) **Religious instruction must be given in the school,** by virtue of S.25 (2).

(*g*) **May withdraw his pupil from such instruction.** – See Chapter II, §4, note (*g*). The same provisions apply to an aided school.

(*h*) **The religious instruction given in the school.** – See S.28 (1). See also notes (*i*) and (*j*) below.

(*i*) **Agreed syllabus instruction.** – See Chapter II, §4, note (*m*) on 'Agreed syllabus'. See also S.28 (1).

(*j*) **In which such instruction is available.** – See S.28 (1).

(*k*) **During the times set apart for religious instruction,** *i.e.* the pupils receiving the agreed syllabus instruction must receive it during the normal time for religious instruction.

(*l*) **The conditions under which.** – See S.25 (5). These conditions are imposed by the Act on all schools. It will be seen, for example, that a pupil may not be withdrawn from a Church of England aided school to receive Church of England religious instruction elsewhere, or from a Roman Catholic aided school to receive Roman Catholic religious instruction elsewhere. Further, if the L.E.A. consider that it would not be unreasonable to make arrangements for agreed syllabus religious instruction, where requested, the arrangements are to be made in the school. But, under the conditions mentioned in S.25 (5) and the text, withdrawal for denominational religious instruction of a different kind from that provided in the school can be arranged.

(*m*) **A pupil must not be required.** – See Chapter II, §4 note (*o*). The same provisions apply in an aided school.

(*n*) **Under the control of the managers or governors.** – See S.28 (1). The managers or governors of an aided denominational school may make arrangements for a clergyman or minister, according to the character of the school, to give religious instruction in the school on any occasion. Such occasions should be entered in the school record.

(*o*) **Arrangements for the inspection of the religious instruction.** – See the proviso to S.77 (5). See also Chapter II, §4, note (*p*); the same provisions apply to an aided school except that the managers or governors as a whole (and not only the foundation managers or foundation governors, as in a controlled school) are concerned.

(*p*) **Inspection of any agreed syllabus instruction.** – See Chapter II, §4, note (*q*). The same provisions apply to an aided school.

# 5. Secular Instruction in an Aided School

Except where otherwise provided in the rules of management or articles of government, the secular instruction in an aided school (*a*) is under the control of the local education authority in the case of a primary school, and is under the control of the governors in the case of a secondary school.

Except where otherwise provided in the rules of management or articles of government, this control includes the power to determine (*b*) the times of the school sessions, the school terms and holidays, and to require attendance at classes in secular instruction held off the school premises.

The authority must not give any directions that will interfere with the provision of reasonable facilities for religious instruction (*c*) in the school during school hours; and the authority must not give directions that will prevent a pupil receiving religious instruction during the hours normally set apart for that purpose (*d*), unless arrangements are made for the pupil to receive religious instruction in the school at some other time.

## NOTES

(*a*) **Secular instruction in an aided school.** – See S.23 (1) and S.23 (2). The rules of management for an aided primary school are made by an order of the L.E.A.; the articles of government for an aided secondary school are made by an order of the Secretary of State. The measure of control delegated to the managers, governors and head teachers is set out in the rules or articles, and S.17 (2) (*b*) particularly requires that the articles shall determine the functions to be exercised by the L.E.A., the governors and the head teacher. See also Chapter II, §5, note (*a*), as to the rights of the L.E.A. and the Secretary of State to inspect maintained schools. The same provisions apply to aided primary and aided secondary schools.

(*b*) **Power to determine.** – See Chapter II, §5, note (*b*). The same provisions apply to aided schools, and it may be added that under S.68 the Secretary of State has also the general power to determine that managers or governors have acted unreasonably and to issue directions accordingly to them.

(*c*) **Reasonable facilities for religious instruction.** – See S.25 (6). Under the *Schools Regulations, 1959*, there must be at least four hours of secular instruction in a school or class mainly for pupils of 8 years of age and over, and at least three hours in a school or class mainly for pupils under 8 years of age.

(*d*) **During the hours normally set apart for that purpose.** – See Chapter II, §5, note (*d*). The same provisions apply to aided schools.

# 6. Teachers in an Aided School

The rules of management of an aided primary school, made by the local education authority, and the articles of government of an aided secondary school, made by the Secretary of State, are to regulate the respective functions (*a*) of the authority, and of the managers or governors, regarding the appointment and dismissal of teachers.

In so doing, the following statutory requirements must be observed (*b*):

### (1) Appointment of Teachers

Teachers in an aided school are to be appointed by the managers or governors (*c*). As the latter are required to provide religious instruction (*d*) in the school in accordance with the provisions of the trust deed, or, where provision for that purpose is not made by such a deed, in accordance with the practice observed before the school became an aided school, they will specifically appoint some teacher or teachers (*e*) to give the required religious instruction as part of their duties.

The number of teachers to be employed in the school is to be determined by the authority.

Provision may be made in the rules or articles (*f*) as agreed between the authority and the managers or governors, or, in default of such agreement, as may be determined by the Secretary of State, to enable the authority to prohibit the appointment, without their consent, of teachers who are to be employed for giving secular instruction; and to enable the authority to give directions as to the educational qualifications of the teachers to be so employed.

### (2) Dismissal of Teachers

The managers or governors have the exclusive right (*g*) to dismiss a teacher who was appointed by them to give religious instruction other than religious instruction in accordance with an agreed syllabus, on the ground that he has failed to give such instruction suitably and efficiently.

Subject to that right of the managers or governors, the rules or articles must make provision to enable the authority to prohibit the dismissal of any teachers without the consent of the authority, and to enable the authority to require the dismissal of any teacher (*h*).

### (3) General Conditions relating to Teachers (*i*)

A teacher in an aided school shall not receive any less emoluments or be deprived of, or disqualified for, any promotion or other advantage by reason of the fact that he gives religious instruction, or by reason of his religious opinions or of his attending religious worship.

### (4) Women Teachers and Marriage

No woman is to be disqualified for employment in an aided school, or be dismissed from such employment, by reason only of marriage (*j*).

NOTES

(*a*) **Are to regulate the respective functions.** – This is laid down in S.24 (2).

(*b*) **The following statutory requirements must be observed.** – See the proviso to S.24 (2).

(*c*) **Are to be appointed by the managers or governors.** – See S.24 (2) (*a*). In the White Paper on *The Principles of Government in Maintained Secondary Schools* the suggestion was made that the head teacher of an aided secondary school might be appointed by the governors after considering the recommendation of a joint committee consisting of a majority of representatives of the governors and of a number of representatives of the L.E.A. The L.E.A. may, therefore, request the Secretary of State to consider making such provision in the articles of government. Similar provision may be made in the case of aided primary schools. But see note (f) below.

All the teachers in an aided school will be employees of the managers or governors, though their salaries will be paid by the L.E.A.

(d) **Are required to provide religious instruction,** by virtue of S.25 (2) and S.28 (1).

(e) **Appoint some teacher or teachers.** – In view of the proviso to S.30 there is nothing to prevent the managers or governors requiring all teachers to satisfy them as to their fitness and competence to give the religious instruction which they, the managers or governors, are required to provide in the school. Where a teacher is specifically appointed to give this religious instruction it is desirable that the agreement with the teacher should contain a clause to that effect. See S.28 (2) and note (g) below.

There is nothing to prevent a teacher from giving agreed syllabus religious instruction, where that is arranged in an aided school, in addition to his giving denominational instruction. It may be arranged to use the agreed syllabus, in some aided schools as the general syllabus, with additional provision for denominational instruction.

(f) **Provision may be made in the rules or articles.** – This is a permissive provision of S.24 (2). See specimen Rules and Articles in the Appendix.

The proviso to S.24 (2) requires the L.E.A. and governors to consult on the provisions to be included in the articles made by the Secretary of State.

(g) **Have the exclusive right.** – This power is contained in S.28 (2). This right is limited by the terms of the Act. See also Chapter II, §6, note (m) – the case of *Smith v. Macnally* applies with equal force to an aided school. Where a teacher is dismissed on the grounds set out in S.28 (2), it is desirable that that fact should appear on the face of the notice given to the teacher.

(h) **To enable the authority to require the dismissal of any teachers.** – This, and the preceding provision of S.24 (2) (a), applies to all aided primary and secondary schools. The articles made by the Secretary of State must contain this power enabling the L.E.A. to prohibit the dismissal of teachers without their consent and enabling the L.E.A. to require the dismissal of any teacher. These powers of the L.E.A. do not prejudice the power of dismissal exclusively exercised by the managers or governors, without the consent of the L.E.A., in the circumstances set out in S.28 (2) and referred to in note (g) above. In all circumstances, the actual dismissal of a teacher in an aided school is by the managers or governors. Where a teacher is dismissed with the consent of or by the requirement of the L.E.A., it is desirable that that fact should appear on the face of the notice given to the teacher. It should be noted that here, as elsewhere, the education committee or sub-committee thereof, if the power has been delegated to them by the L.E.A., may act for the authority and deal with questions concerning the dismissal of teachers in aided schools.

(i) **General conditions relating to teachers.** – These conditions apply to all teachers in an aided school by virtue of the proviso to S.30. Without prejudice to the general application of these conditions, this provision of the Act is particularly addressed to the L.E.A.

(j) **By reason only of marriage.** – See S.24 (3).

# 7. Other Employees at an Aided School

The local education authority may give directions to the managers or governors of an aided school as to the number and conditions of service of persons employed at the school for the care and maintenance of the school premises (a).

Persons employed at an aided school for the school meals service are to be appointed to the staff of the school meals service of the authority (b).

The instrument and rules of management or instrument and articles of government will prescribe the manner of employment of any other employees at an aided school (c). No person is to be disqualified for such employment (d) by reason of his religious opinions, or of his attending or omitting to attend religious worship.

D CVS

### NOTES

(*a*) **Care and maintenance of the school premises,** *i.e.* caretakers, cleaners and grounds-men. The salaries of these employees are paid by the L.E.A. under their duty to maintain the school – see S.114 (2) (*a*). The L.E.A. has the statutory right under S.22 (4) to fix the establishment and conditions of service of these employees.

(*b*) **As regards the staff of an aided school employed for the provision of school meals,** the *Provision of Milk and Meals Regulations, 1945,* require the L.E.A. to employ staff for their school meals service. The L.E.A. may deal centrally with the appoint-ment and dismissal of such staff, but may delegate their powers to the managers or governors to deal with these matters, or to make recommendations thereon to the L.E.A. Expenditure on the salaries and wages of these employees is to be met by the L.E.A. who will fix their conditions of service.

(*c*) **Any other employees at an aided school.** – The clerk to the governors, and correspondent to the managers will be employees of governors or managers. Clerical staff may be employees of the managers or governors, or of the L.E.A., according to the arrangements made. The governors of an aided grammar school, for example, will appoint their clerk for foundation work and the L.E.A. have no responsibility for his salary for such work. The salaries of all these employees for school work will be met by the L.E.A. by virtue of S.114 (2) (*a*), and those salaries and conditions of service will be determined by the L.E.A.

As regards the payment of official expenses of clerks to governors and correspon-dents to managers, etc., see the latter part of note (*b*) of Chapter II, §7, which applies equally to aided schools.

(*d*) **No person is to be disqualified for such employment.** – By virtue of S.30, this includes any employment for the purposes of an aided school, except that of a teacher.

## 8. *Maintenance and Use of Aided School Premises*

The arrangements for meeting the cost of maintaining the school premises of an aided school are as follows. The managers or governors are res-ponsible for external repairs and alterations to the school buildings (*a*), and will receive a maintenance contribution from the Secretary of State (*b*) of 80 per cent of the cost of such repairs and alterations. The local education authority are responsible for (*c*) all internal repairs to the school buildings, and for all repairs and alterations to the other buildings and school grounds. The authority are also responsible for the maintenance of the playing fields and any buildings on them required for use in con-nection therewith. If, during the maintenance of an aided school, front-agers' road charges are to be met in respect of making up streets adjacent to the site and playing fields, the authority must meet those charges. If external repairs to the school buildings are necessary through the use of the buildings for purposes other than those of the school, under a direction or requirement of the authority, the responsibility for those repairs will rest with the authority (*d*).

The authority may direct the managers or governors to provide free of charge (*e*) accommodation on the school premises or any part thereof on any weekday when they are not being used for the purposes of the school, for any educational purpose or youth activities for which the authority desire to provide accommodation; but the authority must be satisfied that there is no suitable alternative accommodation in the area for that purpose, and their power to give such a direction is limited to not more than three days in any week.

Subject to any such directions by the authority and to the statutory requirements of any other Act (*f*), the managers or governors are entitled to control the occupation and use of the premises. The managers or governors are responsible for any expenditure incurred in respect of the use of the school premises by them out of school hours (g), such as the cost of heating and lighting, and any additional payment to the caretaker and groundsman over and above their wages, paid by the authority, for extra duties performed by them for the managers or governors when the premises are so used. They are also responsible for certain insurances (see Chapter VII).

Any sums received by the managers, governors or trustees of the school in respect of the letting or hiring of the school buildings (h) will be retained by them. Any such sums in respect of the letting or hiring of the other buildings and playing fields (i) must be paid over to the authority.

Under the Rating and Valuation Act, 1961, the premises of an aided school are subject to the payment of rates by the authority, not by the managers or governors (j).

## NOTES

(a) **External repairs and alterations to the school buildings.** – This obligation is laid on the managers or governors by S.15 (3)*. For definition of 'school buildings', see Chapter I, §2. For practical details about repairs, see Chapter VII, §10.

Alterations are defined in S.114 (1)*, and include any improvements, enlargements or additions which do not amount to the establishment of a new school. In this context, the alterations are to the school buildings.

(b) **Maintenance contribution from the Secretary of State.** – This duty of the Secretary of State is contained in S.102 as amended by S.1 (1) of the Education Act, 1967.

(c) **The local education authority are responsible for** the list of repairs and upkeep of the premises indicated by virtue of S.15 (3) (b)*. For practical details about repairs see Chapter VII, §10. The L.E.A. have power to carry out repairs in respect of their requirements for the school meals service (see *Provision of Milk and Meals Regulations, 1945*) and the articles of government or rules of management may give the L.E.A. power to carry out other repairs to the school buildings, other buildings, and site, in the case of expenditure for which they are responsible.

(d) **The responsibility for those repairs will rest with the authority**, by virtue of S.15 (3) (b)*.

(e) **May direct the managers or governors to provide, free of charge**, under S.22 (2). This direction also applies, by virtue of S.22 (5), even if the trust deed provides that some person other than managers or governors controls the occupation and use of premises. The L.E.A. are responsible for any expenditure on caretaking, heating, lighting, etc., in connection with such use of the premises by them.

(f) **Statutory requirements of any other Act.** – See S.22 (3), *e.g.* for election purposes. Although the other buildings are part of the premises, the equipment in the school kitchen etc., is the property of the L.E.A. and its use, if any, out of school hours is under the control of the L.E.A. at all times.

(g) **The managers or governors are responsible for any expenditure incurred in respect of the use of the school premises by them out of school hours.** – See S.114 (2) (a). Expenditure incurred through the use of the school premises out of school hours by the managers or governors or by any persons to whom they may let the premises for such use does not fall within the definition of 'expenses of maintaining the school', with which the L.E.A. are solely concerned. The L.E.A. have no power to incur any expenditure on such use of the school premises by the managers or governors or by persons to whom they may let the premises.

(h) **Letting or hiring of the school builders.** – See *S.4 (1)*. For definition of 'school buildings', see Chapter I, §2.

(i) **Letting or hiring of the other buildings and playing fields.** – See *S.4 (1)*. For the definition of 'other buildings' and 'playing fields', see Chapter I, §2. Under the Education Acts, the L.E.A. have to provide and maintain the other buildings and playing fields. But see Chapter III, §1, note (h) concerning the caretaker's house. Where that is provided by the managers or governors, on their own site, they will receive the rent, and the L.E.A. will not be responsible for its maintenance or repair.

(j) **Premises of an aided school are subject to rates.** – See Chapter II, §8, note (h).

# IV. THE SPECIAL AGREEMENT SCHOOL

## 1. *Special Agreement Schools*

Proposals for about five hundred voluntary senior public elementary schools were submitted to local education authorities under the Education Act, 1936, but only thirty-seven were carried out under that Act, because of the war, before April 1st, 1945. The Education Act, 1944, repealed the whole of the 1936 Act, but made provision, in the Third Schedule to the Act, for the revival of proposals that had lapsed through the time limit set by the previous Act. As a result, about one hundred and fifty special agreement schools (*a*) have been established under the Education Act, 1944. But the financial advantages to the proposers of establishing special agreement schools rather than aided schools has since disappeared (*b*); and as, in other respects (*c*), it is more advantageous to proposers to establish an aided school than a special agreement school, they will, except as mentioned in paragraph 2 below, choose the former.

NOTES

(*a*) **Special agreement schools.** – The term 'special agreement' was first used and defined in the Education Act, 1944, in S.114 (1), as an agreement made under the Third Schedule to the Act. Under the Education Act, 1936, the voluntary schools then concerned were given no special name, and proposals under that Act provided for new voluntary schools for senior pupils, or for enlarging voluntary public elementary schools to provide or improve the accommodation for seniors. Special agreement schools established under the Education Act, 1944, are secondary schools.

(*b*) **Has since disappeared.** – Under the Education Act, 1944, proposers of a special agreement school could receive a grant from the L.E.A. of 75 per cent of their expenditure on the provision of the site and school buildings of the school, compared with a grant of 50 per cent from the Minister towards the corresponding costs of an aided school. The Education Act, 1959, raised the latter grant to 75 per cent, and now the Education Act, 1967, has increased it to 80 per cent for all aided schools whose establishment is approved.

(*c*) **In other respects.** – The powers of governors of an aided secondary school are greater than those of a special agreement school, as may be seen by comparing the corresponding paragraphs of Chapters III and IV of this book.

## 2. *Capital Expenditure on School Premises*

Capital expenditure on the premises of a special agreement school will, in practice, be limited in future, because of the grant facilities now available for aided schools, to the following two cases: **1** the alteration of the premises of an existing school; **2** the alteration of the premises of a school to such an extent as to amount to the establishment of a new school. The provisions of the Education Acts for each of these cases are given below:

### (1) **Alteration of an Existing Special Agreement School**

The governors are responsible for the capital expenditure on the following alterations (*a*) to the premises (*b*) of an existing special agreement school: the improvement or enlargement (*c*) of, or addition to, the school buildings (*d*). Towards this expenditure the Secretary of State will make a maintenance contribution of 80 per cent (e). Any other capital expenditure on the premises, such as an addition to the existing site (f), the improvement of the school grounds (g), frontagers' road charges, the alteration or provision of other buildings (h), or the provision or extension of playing fields, and boundary walls or fence to such fields (i), is to be met by the local education authority.

The authority must convey their interest in any addition to the site, and in any buildings thereon which are to form part of the school premises, to the trustees of the school (j); but the legitimate interests of the authority and of the Secretary of State are protected in the event of the discontinuance of the school by the governors (k), and if part or the whole of the premises are acquired from the trustees by any person (l). Any playing fields provided by the authority and any buildings on them provided by the authority, for use in connection therewith, remain the property of the authority (m). The authority may carry out this work (n).

## (2) Enlargement of an Existing Special Agreement School to the extent of establishing a New School

An existing special agreement school may be enlarged to such an extent as to amount to the establishment of a new school (o). Any alterations or additions to the site, to the school grounds, and to the school buildings, required for the enlargement, and any road charges in respect of the site thereby involved, must be paid for by the governors (p), who will receive a grant of 80 per cent (q) of their approved expenditure thereon from the Secretary of State. The local education authority must provide the other buildings (r) on the site required for the enlarged school, which, being built on the site belonging to the school trustees, become their property. The legitimate interests of the authority and of the Secretary of State are protected in the event of the discontinuance of the school by the governors (s).

The authority must also provide any additions to the playing fields (t) required for the enlarged school, the boundary walls or fence to such fields, and any buildings on them required for use in connection therewith. The authority may carry out this work (u), and the additions to the playing fields and any buildings on them provided by the authority for use in connection therewith, remain the property of the authority (v).

### NOTES

(a) **Alterations** are defined in S.114 (1)* as improvements, enlargements or additions to the school premises that do not amount to the establishment of a new school. See S.67 (4), and note (b) below. In so far as alterations are to the school buildings (see Chapter I, §2) the expenditure is the responsibility of the governors by S.15 (3)*.

(b) **Premises.** – For definition see Chapter I, §2.

(c) **Enlargement.** – That is, an enlargement that does not amount to the establishment of a new school. See S.114 (1)* and S.67 (4). An enlargement of up to 25 per cent is not regarded as the establishment of a new school.

(d) **School buildings.** – See Chapter I, §2.

(e) **Eighty per cent.** – By S.102 as amended by S.1 (1) of the Education Act, 1967.

(f) **Addition to the existing site.** – The duty of the L.E.A. to provide is set out in *S.3* and *§1 of the First Schedule.* Any expenditure on the addition to the site to make it suitable for building purposes must, by *§3 of the First Schedule,* be met by the L.E.A. If such an addition has any buildings on it that are of value for the school buildings, that will be debited to the governors, by §4 *of the First Schedule*, since it is their duty to provide the school buildings.

(g) **School grounds.** – See Chapter I, §2.

(h) **Other buildings.** – See Chapter I, §2 – *i.e.* buildings which by *S.4* are not school buildings. The alteration of these other buildings is not included in the duties of the governors by S.15 (3)* and is, therefore, the duty of the L.E.A.under their maintenance of the school – see S.114 (2) (*a*). If a caretaker's house is provided on the site, it is an other building. If the L.E.A. build this house, the rent is to be paid over to them by *S.4 (1)*, and they are responsible for its maintenance. The caretaker at a special agreement school is an employee of the L.E.A.

(i) **Playing fields.** – See Chapter II, §1, note (*e*). The same duty applies here.

(j) **Trustees of the school.** – See Chapter II, §1, note (*i*). The provisions of the Act, referred to in that note, apply also to the circumstances of an altered special agreement school.

(k) **Discontinuance of the school by the governors.** – See Chapter II, §1, note (*j*). The same provisions apply to the case of an altered special agreement school.

(l) **If part or the whole of the premises are acquired from the trustees by any person.** – See Chapter II, §1, note (*k*). The same provisions apply in the case of a special agreement school.

(m) **Playing fields remain the property of the authority.** – See Chapter II, §1, note (*m*). The same provisions apply in the case of a special agreement school.

(n) **Authority may carry out this work.** – See Chapter III, §1, note (*n*). The same provisions apply in the case of a special agreement school.

(o) **To such an extent as to amount to the establishment of a new school.** – If the enlargement increases the recognized accommodation of the school by more than 25 per cent, the Secretary of State will determine under S.67 (4) that it amounts to the establishment of a new school. The enlargement will involve a proposal under S.13 (2) and the publication of notices.

(p) **Must be paid for by the governors.** – By virtue of S.13 (7)*, coupled with *S.3 and sub-paragraph (a) of the proviso to §1 of the First Schedule.*

(q) **Will receive a grant of 80 per cent.** – Under S.1 (2) (*b*) of the Education Act, 1967.

(r) **L.E.A. must provide the other buildings.** – In the case of a new special agreement school, the duty of the L.E.A. to provide the other buildings is laid down in S.13 (7)*. There is no obligation on the L.E.A. to provide a caretaker's house, and they may prefer to leave that provision to the governors.

(s) **In the event of the discontinuance of the school by the governors.** – See Chapter II, §1, note (*j*). The same provisions apply here in respect of capital expenditure incurred by the L.E.A. and in respect of the capital grants made by the Secretary of State.

(t) **Any additions to the playing fields.** – The L.E.A. must provide the items mentioned here by virtue of S.13 (7)*.

(u) **Authority may carry out this work.** – Because they are responsible for their provision, and they are the owners of such parts of the premises.

(v) **Remain the property of the authority.** – Because they are provided by the L.E.A. and are excluded from the definition of site (which is the property of the school trustees) in *S.16 (1)*.

# 3. *Instrument and Articles of Government of a Special Agreement School*

The instrument of government (*a*) of a special agreement secondary school, which provides for the constitution of the body of governors, is made by an order of the Secretary of State (*b*). The number of governors is determined after consultation with the local education authority, but two-thirds must be foundation governors (*c*) and one-third must be governors appointed by the authority (*d*).

The articles of government (*e*) are made by an order of the Secretary of State. These articles govern the conduct of the school, subject to the provisions of the Education Acts and of any trust deed of the school (*f*), and the articles must, in particular, define the functions to be exercised by the authority, the governors and the head teacher.

If the Secretary of State considers that anything included or proposed to be included in the instrument or articles of government is inconsistent with the trust deed, and if he thinks it is just and expedient, in the interests of the school, that the trust deed should be modified (g) to remove the inconsistency, he may make an order modifying the trust deed. But before doing so, he is bound to give an opportunity to the authority and to any other persons who appear to him to be concerned with the government of the school, to make representations to him; and he must have regard to all the circumstances of the school, and, in the case of an existing school, to the manner in which it has previously been conducted.

Specimen instrument and articles of government for a special agreement secondary school are given in the Appendix.

### NOTES

(a) **Instrument of government.** – See Chapter III, §3, note (a). As in the case of an aided school, all matters coming within the purview of the governors of a special agreement school stand referred to the whole of the governors, subject to the exception in the case of the special agreement school, that questions relating to the appointment of a reserved teacher and to his dismissal as a reserved teacher stand referred to the foundation governors only, in the manner described in §7 (1) of this Chapter, and the relevant notes thereon.

(b) **Order of the Secretary of State.** – See S.17 (2).

(c) **Foundation governors.** – See Chapter II, §2, note (d). The same provisions apply to foundation governors. See also S.19 (2) (b).

(d) **Governors appointed by the authority.** – See S.19 (2) (b). The total number of governors, foundation and authority governors, must be a multiple of three.

(e) **Articles of government.** – See Chapter II, §3, note (e).

(f) **Trust deed of the school.** – See Chapter II, §3, note (f).

(g) **That the trust deed should be modified.** – See Chapter II, §3, note (g).

## 4. Religious Worship and Religious Instruction in a Special Agreement School

The school day in a special agreement school must begin with collective worship (a) for all pupils, except those who have been withdrawn (b) from such worship by their parents. Except on any special occasion (c), the religious worship must take place on the school premises, and, unless the governors consider that the premises make the arrangement impracticable, a single act of worship must be arranged (d).

The Education Acts do not specify the character of the religious worship (e) in a special agreement school, but it is under the control of the governors, subject to any provisions of the special agreement and the articles of government.

Religious instruction must be given in the school (f), but a parent may withdraw his pupil from such instruction (g), or may withdraw his pupil from the school in order to receive religious instruction, of a kind not provided in the school, elsewhere.

The religious instruction given in the school (h) must be in accordance with the trust deed relating to the school, or, where provision for that purpose is not made by such a deed, in accordance with the practice observed before the school became a special agreement school.

If, however, the parents of pupils desire them to receive agreed syllabus instruction (*i*), and if the pupils cannot with reasonable convenience attend a school in which such instruction is available (*j*), then, unless the authority are satisfied that owing to special circumstances it would be unreasonable to do so, arrangements must be made for agreed syllabus instruction for those pupils in the school during the times set apart for religious instruction (*k*). These arrangements must ordinarily be made by the governors, but if the authority are satisfied that the governors are unwilling to make the arrangements, the authority must make the arrangements themselves.

The conditions under which (*l*) a pupil may be withdrawn from the school by his parents in order to receive religious instruction of a kind not provided in the school, elsewhere, are as follows: (i) the authority must be satisfied that the pupil cannot reasonably attend a school at which the desired religious instruction is given; (ii) the authority must be satisfied that arrangements have, in fact, been made for the pupil to receive the desired religious instruction elsewhere; (iii) the withdrawal of the pupil can only be made at the beginning or at the end of the school session, and only for such periods as are reasonably necessary.

A pupil must not be required (*m*), as a condition of attending the school, either to attend or to abstain from attending a Sunday School or a place of religious worship.

The religious instruction given in a special agreement school is to be under the control of the governors (*n*). Except as regards any agreed syllabus instruction given in the school, the arrangements for the inspection of the religious instruction (*o*) are to be made by the governors. The inspection of any agreed syllabus (*p*) given in a special agreement school may only be carried out by the following persons: (i) one of H.M. Inspectors; (ii) a person appointed by the Secretary of State as an additional inspector and ordinarily employed for the purpose of inspecting secular instruction; (iii) an officer in the full-time employment of the authority who is ordinarily employed for the purpose of inspecting secular instruction.

## NOTES

(*a*) **Must begin with collective worship,** by virtue of S.25 (1).

(*b*) **Except those who have been withdrawn.** – See Chapter II, §4, note (*b*). The same provisions apply to a special agreement school. A parent's withdrawal of his pupil from religious worship also applies to the special occasions (see note (*c*) below) on which the worship is held elsewhere than on the school premises.

(*c*) **Except on any special occasion.** – See Chapter III, §4, note (*c*). The same provisions apply to a special agreement school.

(*d*) **A single act of worship must be arranged.** – See S.25 (1).

(*e*) **Character of the religious worship.** – Subject to any provisions of the special agreement and the articles of government relating to the matter, the religious worship is under the control of the governors.

If the governors so decide, a priest or minister, according to the denomination of the school, may conduct the religious worship on any occasion. Such occasions should be entered in the school record.

(*f*) **Religious instruction must be given in the school,** by virtue of S.25 (2).

(*g*) **May withdraw his pupil from such instruction.** – See S.25 (4) and Chapter II, §4 note (*g*). The same provisions apply in a special agreement school.

(*h*) **The religious instruction given in the school.** – See S.28 (1). See also notes (*j*) and (*k*) below.

(*i*) **Agreed syllabus instruction.** – See Chapter II, §4, note (*m*) on 'Agreed syllabus'. See also S.28 (1).

(*j*) **In which such instruction is available.** – See S.28 (1).

(*k*) **During the time set apart for religious instruction,** *i.e.* the pupils receiving the agreed syllabus instruction must receive it during the normal times for religious instruction.

(*l*) **The conditions under which.** – See S.25 (5). These conditions are imposed by the Act on all schools. See also Chapter III, §4, note (*l*). The same provisions apply to a special agreement school.

(*m*) **A pupil must not be required.** – See Chapter II, §4, note (*o*). The same provisions apply in a special agreement school.

(*n*) **Under the control of the governors.** – See S.28 (1). The governors may make arrangements for a priest or minister, according to the character of the school, to give religious instruction in the school on any occasion. Such occasions should be entered in the school record.

(*o*) **Arrangements for the inspection of the religious instruction.** – See the proviso to S.77 (5). See also Chapter II, §4, note (*p*). The same provisions apply to a special agreement school, except that the governors as a whole (and not only the foundation governors as in a controlled school) are concerned.

(*p*) **Inspection of any agreed syllabus instruction.** – See Chapter II, §4, note (*q*). The same provisions apply to a special agreement school.

# 5. *Secular Instruction in a Special Agreement School*

Except where otherwise provided in the articles of government, the secular instruction in a special agreement secondary school (*a*) is under the control of the local education authority. This control includes the power to determine (*b*) the times of the school sessions, the school terms, holidays, and to require attendance at classes in secular instruction held off the school premises.

The authority must not give any directions that will interfere with the provision of reasonable facilities for religious instruction (*c*) in the school during school hours; and the authority must not give directions that will prevent a pupil receiving religious instruction during the hours normally set apart for that purpose (*d*), unless arrangements are made for the pupil to receive religious instruction in the school at some other time.

### NOTES

(*a*) **Secular instruction in a special agreement school.** – See S.23 (1). The articles of government for a special agreement secondary school are made by an order of the Secretary of State. The measure of control delegated to the governors and head teacher is set out in the articles and S.17 (3) (*b*) particularly requires that the articles shall determine the functions to be exercised by the L.E.A., the governors and the head teacher. See also Chapter II, §5, note (*a*), as to the rights of the L.E.A. and the Secretary of State to inspect maintained schools. The same provisions apply to the special agreement secondary school.

(*b*) **Power to determine.** – See Chapter II, §5, note (*b*). The same provisions apply to special agreement schools.

(*c*) **Reasonable facilities for religious instruction.** – See S.25 (6). If the governors of a special agreement school desire to arrange that all pupils shall have religious instruction daily, the illustration given in Chapter II, §5, note (*c*), for a controlled school could be applied equally well by the L.E.A. to the special agreement secondary school.

(*d*) **During the hours normally set apart for that purpose.** – See Chapter II, §5, note (*d*). The same provisions apply to special agreement schools.

# 6. *Teachers in a Special Agreement School*

Subject to the powers of the foundation governors concerning the appointment of reserved teachers, referred to below, the appointment of all teachers in a special agreement school is under the control of the local education authority (*a*), except in so far as such control is delegated to the governors (*b*) under the articles of government for the school.

No teacher in a special agreement school may be dismissed except by the authority (*c*).

Other special and general conditions concerning the appointment and dismissal of teachers in a special agreement school are given below:

### (1) Reserved Teachers

A reserved teacher (*d*) is a person selected for his fitness and competence to give religious instruction in accordance with the provisions of the special agreement and articles of government, and who is specifically appointed to give such instruction (*e*).

The number of the teaching staff who are to be reserved teachers (*f*) is to be specified in the agreement made between the authority and the proposers under the Third Schedule to the Education Act, 1944.

The authority must consult the foundation governors (*g*) before any person is appointed as a reserved teacher in the special agreement school, and unless the foundation governors are satisfied that the person is fit and competent to give the required religious instruction (*h*), the authority must not appoint that person as a reserved teacher in that school (*i*).

If the foundation governors consider that any reserved teacher has failed to give the required religious instruction efficiently and suitably, they may require the authority to dismiss him from employment as a reserved teacher in the school (*j*).

### (2) General Conditions relating to Reserved Teachers (*k*)

A reserved teacher shall not receive any less emolument or be deprived of, or disqualified for, any promotion or other advantage by reason of the fact that he gives religious instruction, or by reason of his religious opinions or of his attending religious worship.

### (3) General Conditions relating to Non-Reserved Teachers (*l*)

No person is to be disqualified from being a teacher, other than a reserved teacher, in a special agreement school, by reason of his religious opinions, or of his attending or omitting to attend religious worship (*m*). No such teacher (*n*) shall be required to give religious instruction (*o*), or receive any less emolument or be deprived of, or disqualified for, any promotion or other advantage by reason of the fact that he does or does not give religious instruction, or by reason of his religious opinions, or of his attending or omitting to attend religious worship.

### (4) Women Teachers and Marriage

No woman is to be disqualified for employment as a teacher in a special agreement school, or be dismissed from such employment, by reason only of marriage (*p*).

### NOTES

(*a*) **Under the control of the local education authority.** – See S.24 (1). This control is comprehensive, subject to the powers of the foundation governors concerning the appointment of reserved teachers, and subject to the conditions laid down by the Act. All teachers in a special agreement school are employees of the L.E.A. The L.E.A. may fix the number of teachers to be employed in a school, and may appoint the teachers subject to any powers delegated to the governors under the articles of government for the school.

(b) **Except in so far as such control is delegated to the governors.** – See S.24 (1). The articles of government for a special agreement school are made by the Secretary of State, who thereby determines, among other things, what measure of the control exercised by the L.E.A. over the appointment of teachers shall be delegated to the governors. The articles, for example, may require the L.E.A. to appoint the head teacher on the recommendation of a joint committee consisting of an equal number of representatives of the L.E.A. and of the governors.

The articles may also require that the assistant teachers in a special agreement school shall be appointed by the governors, subject, possibly, to the right of the L.E.A. to fill a vacancy by transferring a teacher from another school in their area, or from a group of new entrants to the teaching profession appointed by the L.E.A. to their service.

(c) **No teacher in a special agreement school shall be dismissed except by the authority.** – This is laid down in S.24 (1). For the conditions under which the foundation governors may require the L.E.A. to dismiss a reserved teacher, see note (j) below. The articles of government of a special agreement school may require the L.E.A. to consult the governors before dismissing a teacher and may provide that the governors shall be entitled to recommend the dismissal of a teacher. It should be noted that here, as elsewhere, the education committee or a sub-committee thereof, if the power has been delegated to them by the L.E.A., may act for the authority and deal with the dismissal of teachers.

(d) **Reserved teacher.** – See S.28 (3) coupled with §7 of the Third Schedule.

(e) **Who is specifically appointed to give such instruction.** – The minute of appointment or contract of service should specifically state that the teacher is appointed as a reserved teacher, and may particularize the requirement to be fulfilled or the undertaking to be given by the teacher.

A reserved teacher may also give agreed syllabus instruction if he is prepared to do so.

(f) **Number of the teaching staff who are to be reserved teachers.** – See §7 of the Third Schedule. The proportion of reserved teachers in a special agreement school may be subsequently varied by agreement between the L.E.A. and the governors, by virtue of §8 of the Third Schedule. The head teacher will be a reserved teacher. Most of the assistant teachers will similarly be reserved teachers, though the proportion will vary according to local circumstances, e.g. the proportion of the pupils whose parents belong to the religious body establishing the school. Teachers appointed for practical subjects may well be specified as persons who are not reserved teachers. All these points are matters to be specified in the agreement.

(g) **The authority must consult the foundation governors,** by virtue of S.28 (3). The articles of government of a special agreement school may provide for the appointment of a reserved teacher by the governors after the foundation governors have expressed themselves satisfied that the person is fit and competent to give the required religious instruction. The L.E.A. before confirming the appointment or entering into the written agreement with the reserved teacher, must be satisfied that the foundation governors have been consulted and have not declared themselves dissatisfied with the proposed appointment. If the L.E.A. directly appoint any teacher in a special agreement school, they must consult the foundation governors before making the appointment of a reserved teacher for that school.

(h) **Required religious instruction.** – See S.28 (3) and §7 of the Third Schedule to the Act.

(i) **Must not appoint that person as a reserved teacher in that school.** – The foundation governors can veto the proposed appointment of a reserved teacher on the grounds mentioned in S.28 (3). This does not necessarily preclude the appointment of that person as a non-reserved teacher in that school or as a reserved teacher in another school.

(j) **Dismiss him from employment as a reserved teacher in that school.** – See S.28 (4). See Chapter II, §6, note (m). The same applies to a reserved teacher in a special agreement school.

(*k*) **General conditions relating to reserved teachers.** – See Chapter II, §6, note (*t*). The same provisions apply to reserved teachers in a special agreement school.

(*l*) **General conditions relating to non-reserved teachers.** – See Chapter II, §6, note (*p*). The same provisions apply to non-reserved teachers in a special agreement school.

(*m*) **Attending or omitting to attend religious worship,** *i.e.* in a school or elsewhere.

(*n*) **No such teacher,** *i.e.* a teacher who is not a reserved teacher.

(*o*) **No such teacher shall be required to give religious instruction.** – See Chapter II, §6, note (*s*). The same provisions apply to a special agreement school.

(*p*) **By reason only of marriage.** – See S.24 (3).

# 7. *Other Employees in a Special Agreement School*

Other persons (*a*) employed for the purposes of a special agreement school, subject to the exception of the clerk to the governors (*b*), are appointed and dismissed by the authority (*c*). The authority also determine their conditions of service.

No person is to be disqualified for such employment (*d*) by reason of his religious opinions, or of his attending or omitting to attend religious worship.

### NOTES

(*a*) **Other persons,** *e.g.* caretakers, cleaners, groundsmen – see S.22 (4); clerical staff, school meals staff.

(*b*) **Clerk to the governors.** – It is the practice of the Secretary of State to provide in the articles of government for the clerk to be appointed and dismissed by the governors. The L.E.A. will determine the conditions of service of the clerk, so far as his duties concern the maintenance of the school, and will remunerate him accordingly – see S.114 (2) (*a*). The L.E.A. are also responsible for the official expenses incurred by the clerk to the governors with respect to his duties relating to the maintenance of the school.

(*c*) **To be appointed and dismissed by the authority.** – The articles of government may provide for the delegation of the power of appointment and dismissal to the governors, or of recommending appointment and dismissal to the L.E.A. As regards school meals staff, the *Provision of Milk and Meals Regulations, 1945*, require their appointment to the service of the L.E.A.

(*d*) **For such employment.** – Disqualification on religious grounds for any of the employments referred to in notes (*a*) and (*b*) above, is prohibited by S.30.

# 8. *Maintenance and Use of Special Agreement School Premises*

The arrangements for meeting the cost of maintaining the school premises of a special agreement school are as follows. The governors are responsible for external repairs and alterations to the school buildings (*a*), and will receive a maintenance contribution from the Secretary of State (*b*) of 80 per cent of the cost of such repairs. The local education authority are responsible for (*c*) all internal repairs to the school buildings, and all repairs to the other buildings and to the school grounds. The authority are also responsible for the maintenance of the playing fields and for repairs to any buildings on them required for use in connection therewith. If external repairs to the school buildings are necessary through the use of the buildings for purposes other than those of the school, under a direction or requirement of the authority, the responsibility for those repairs will rest with the authority (*d*).

The authority may direct the governors to provide free of charge (*e*) accommodation on the school premises or any part thereof on any weekday when they are not being used for the purposes of the school, for any educational purpose or youth activities for which the authority desire to provide accommodation; but the authority must be satisfied that there is no suitable alternative accommodation in the area for that purpose, and their power to direct the use of the premises is limited to not more than three days in any week.

Subject to any such directions by the authority and to the statutory requirements of any other Act $(f)$, the governors are entitled to control the occupation and use of the premises.

The governors are responsible for any expenditure incurred in respect of the use of the school premises by them out of school hours $(g)$, such as the cost of heating and lighting, and any additional payment to the caretaker and groundsman over and above their wages, paid by the authority, for extra duties performed by them for the governors when the premises are so used. They are also responsible for certain insurances (see Chapter VII).

Any sums received by the governors or trustees of the school in respect of the letting or hiring of the school buildings $(h)$ will be retained by them. Any such sums in respect of the letting or hiring of the other buildings and playing fields $(i)$ must be paid over to the authority.

Under the Rating and Valuation Act, 1961, the premises of a special agreement school are subject to the payment of rates by the authority, not by the managers or governors $(j)$.

## NOTES

(a) **External repairs and alterations to the school buildings.** – See Chapter III, §8, note (a). The same provisions apply to a special agreement school. For practical details, see Chapter VII.

(b) **Maintenance contribution from the Secretary of State.** – See Chapter III, §8, note (b). The same provisions apply to a special agreement school.

(c) **The local education authority are responsible for.** – See Chapter III, §8, note (c). The same provisions apply to a special agreement school For practical details about repairs see §10 of Chapter VII. The L.E.A. have power to carry out repairs in respect of their requirements for the school meals service (see *Provision of Milk and Meals Regulations, 1945*) and the articles of government may give the L.E.A. power to carry out other repairs to the school buildings, other buildings, and site, in the case of expenditure for which they are responsible.

(d) **The responsibility for those repairs will rest with the authority,** by virtue of S.15 (3) (b)*.

(e) **May direct the governors to provide free of charge.** – See Chapter III, §8, note (e). The same provisions apply to a special agreement school.

(f) **Statutory requirements of any other Act.** – See Chapter III, §8, note (f). The same arrangements apply to a special agreement school.

(g) **The governors are responsible for any expenditure incurred in respect of the use of the school premises by them out of school hours.** – See Chapter III, §8, note (g). The same arrangements apply to a special agreement school and for the same reasons.

(h) **Letting or hiring of the school buildings.** – See *S.4 (1)*. For definition of 'school buildings', see Chapter I, §2.

(i) **Letting or hiring of the other buildings and playing fields.** – See *S.4 (1)*. For the definition of 'other buildings' and 'playing fields', see Chapter I, §2. Under the Education Acts the L.E.A. have to provide and maintain the other buildings and playing fields. If the L.E.A. provide a caretaker's house, they will receive the rent for it and be responsible for its maintenance. If the governors provide a caretaker's house on their own site, they will receive the rent, and the L.E.A. will not be responsible for its maintenance.

(j) **Premises of a special agreement school are subject to rates.** – See Chapter II, §8, note (h).

# V. THE COUNTY SCHOOL

## 1. *Capital Expenditure on School Premises*

Capital expenditure on the premises of county schools under the Education Acts may be involved in one of the three following ways: 1 the alteration of the premises of an existing school (*a*); 2 the transfer of an existing school to a new site (*b*); 3 the establishment of a new county school (*c*). In all cases the whole of the capital expenditure involved will be met by the local education authority without specific grant from the Secretary of State (*d*).

### NOTES

(*a*) **Alterations of the premises of an existing school.** – For the definition of alteration see S.114 (1)*.

(*b*) **Transfer of an existing school to a new site.** – The conditions under which an existing county school may be transferred to a new site are set out in S.16 (1). A transfer may be made because it is not reasonably practicable to alter the existing premises to conform with the standards prescribed under the Act, or because of any movement of population, or because of any action taken or proposed to be taken under the Housing Acts or the Town and Country Planning Acts. For definition of site, see Chapter I, §2.

(*c*) **Establishment of a new county school,** that is to say, of a new entity, essentially different from an existing school. In case of doubt as to whether the alteration of an existing school constitutes the establishment of a new school the question is one for determination by the Minister under S.67 (4). If the alteration is to provide accommodation for an increase in the number of pupils of more than 25 per cent the Secretary of State will regard it as amounting to the establishment of a new school. Other examples of the establishment of new county schools are as follows: 1 a new secondary school for the reorganization of schools into primary and secondary schools; 2 a new school for a new housing estate, if the scheme does not simply involve the transfer of the pupils and their school from old to new school premises.

(*d*) **Without specific grant from the Secretary of State.** – Under the Local Government Act, 1966, rate support grants are made by the Minister of Housing and Local Government towards the expenditure of local authorities on the various services they provide, but, except in the case of certain services, of which education is not one, no specific grants are made to local authorities.

## 2. *Instrument and Rules of Management of a County Primary School*

The instrument of management (*a*) of a county primary school, which provides for the constitution of the body of managers, is made by an order of the local education authority (*b*). In the administrative area of a county, the number of the managers, subject to a minimum of six, is determined by the authority (*c*), two-thirds of whom are to be appointed by the authority (*d*) and one-third by the minor authority (*e*). In a county borough the authority determine the constitution of the body of managers (*f*).

The rules of management (*g*) are made by an order of the authority. These rules govern the conduct of the school subject to the provisions of the Education Acts (*h*).

### NOTES

(*a*) **Instrument of management.** – See S.17 (1). The instrument, besides fixing the constitution and method of appointment of the managers, in accordance with the provisions of the Education Acts, also regulates the proceedings of the managers, in accordance with S.21 and the Fourth Schedule as amended by the Education (Miscellaneous Provisions) Act, 1948.

Special provision for the grouping of two or more county schools under one managing body (or for two or more county and voluntary schools with the consent of the voluntary school managers) may be made. For details of such arrangements, see S.20.

(b) **Order of the local education authority.** – See S.17 (2).

(c) **Is determined by the authority,** by virtue of S.18 (1).

(d) **Two-thirds of whom are to be appointed by the authority,** by virtue of S.18 (1). If there are six managers, the composition will be four L.E.A., two minor authority. If nine, six L.E.A., three minor authority, and so on.

(e) **Minor authority.** – See Chapter II, §2, note (e).

(f) **Determine the constitution of the body of managers,** by virtue of S.18 (2). There is no minor authority in the area of a county borough – see definition of minor authority in S.114 (1).

(g) **Rules of management.** – See S.17 (3) (a).

(h) **Subject to the provisions of the Education Acts.** – By S.17 (3) the rules must be made by the L.E.A.

## 3. *Instrument and Articles of Government of a County Secondary School*

The instrument of government (a) of a county secondary school, which provides for the constitution of the body of governors, is made by an order of the local education authority (b). The number of governors and the manner of their appointment are to be determined by the authority (c) The articles of government (d) are made by an order of the authority and approved by the Secretary of State (e). These articles govern the conduct of the school, subject to the provisions of the Education Acts, and the articles must, in particular, define the functions to be exercised by the authority, the governors and the head teacher.

### NOTES

(a) **Instrument of government.** – See S.17 (1) and Chapter V, §2, note (a). The same provisions, *mutatis mutandis*, apply to a county secondary school.

(b) **Order of the local education authority.** – See S.17 (2).

(c) **Are to be determined by the authority,** by virtue of S.19 (1).

(d) **Articles of government.** – See S.17 (3) (b). See also Chapter II, §3, note (e).

(e) **Approved by the Secretary of State.** – See S.17 (3) (b). For a county primary school, the rules of management, made by the L.E.A., do not require the Secretary of State's approval. But the corresponding articles of government for a county secondary school do.

## 4. *Religious Worship and Religious Instruction in a County School*

The school day in a county school must begin with collective worship (a) for all pupils, except those who have been withdrawn (b) from such worship by their parents. The religious worship must take place on the school premises (c) and, unless the local education authority consider that the premises make the arrangement impracticable, a single act of worship must be arranged (d).

The religious worship in a county school must not be distinctive of any particular religious denomination (e).

Religious instruction, in accordance with an agreed syllabus (*f*) and not including any catechism or formulary (*g*) distinctive of any particular religious denomination, must be given in a county school; but a parent may withdraw his pupil from such instruction (*h*), or may withdraw his pupil from the school in order to receive religious instruction, of a kind not provided in the school, elsewhere (*i*).

If a county secondary school is so situated that arrangements cannot conveniently be made for the withdrawal of pupils by their parents, in accordance with the provisions of the Act, to receive religious instruction elsewhere, the authority must provide facilities (*j*) on the school premises, unless they are satisfied that, owing to special circumstances, it would be unreasonable to do so (*k*).

If a pupil is withdrawn from the school by his parents in order to receive religious instruction, of a kind not provided in the school, elsewhere, the following conditions must be observed (*l*): (i) the authority must be satisfied that the pupil cannot reasonably attend a school at which the desired religious instruction is given; (ii) the authority must be satisfied that arrangements have, in fact, been made for the pupil to receive the desired religious instruction elsewhere; (iii) the withdrawal of the pupil must only be made either at the beginning or at the end of the school session, and only for such periods as are reasonably necessary.

A pupil must not be required (*m*), as a condition of attending the school, either to attend or to abstain from attending a Sunday School or a place of religious worship.

The inspection of religious instruction given in a county school (*n*) may only be carried out by one of the following persons: (i) one of H.M. Inspectors; (ii) a person appointed by the Secretary of State as an additional inspector and ordinarily employed for the purpose of inspecting secular instruction; (iii) an officer in the full-time employment of the authority who is ordinarily employed for the purpose of inspecting secular instruction.

## NOTES

(*a*) **Must begin with collective worship,** by virtue of S.25 (1).

(*b*) **Except those who have been withdrawn.** – See Chapter II, §4, note (*b*). The same provisions apply to a county school.

(*c*) **Must take place on the school premises,** by virtue of *S.7 (1)*.

(*d*) **A single act of worship must be arranged.** – See S.25 (1).

(*e*) **Must not be distinctive of any particular religious denomination.** – See S.26.

(*f*) **Agreed syllabus.** – See Chapter II, §4, note (*m*).

(*g*) **Not including any catechism or formulary.** – See S.26, which re-enacts again the Cowper-Temple clause of the Elementary Education Act, 1870.

(*h*) **May withdraw his pupil from such instruction.** – See Chapter II, §4, note (*g*). The same provisions apply to a county school.

(*i*) **In order to receive religious instruction of a kind which is not provided in the school, elsewhere.** – Under S.25 (5) a pupil may be withdrawn by his parent from religious worship, or religious instruction, or from both, in order to receive religious instruction, of a kind not provided in the school, elsewhere. The approval of the L.E.A. must first be obtained and the conditions set out in S.25 (5) and the text must be fulfilled.

(*j*) **The authority must provide facilities.** – This duty is laid down in the proviso to S.26, which applies only to county secondary schools. This arrangement, under which the L.E.A. are to provide facilities, *e.g.* on the school premises, is subject to certain limiting conditions, set out in S.26, namely: (i) withdrawal to receive the religious instruction elsewhere cannot conveniently be made. That does not mean that withdrawal to a church is inconvenient. What has to be shown is that withdrawal to other premises cannot conveniently be made, not that it would involve cost in renting or heating the premises. This provision was made in response to a demand for facilities where the county school was in an isolated position – at 'the cross roads'; (ii) the L.E.A. must be satisfied that the parents of pupils attending the school desire them to receive denominational instruction; (iii) satisfactory arrangements must have been made, without cost to the L.E.A., for such instruction to those pupils in the school.

(*k*) **It would be unreasonable to do so.** – There may be special circumstances in a particular case that would make it unreasonable to provide the necessary facilities for this denominational instruction. The L.E.A. must act reasonably in reaching such a conclusion or the Secretary of State can rule against them under S.68.

(*l*) **The following conditions must be observed.** – See S.25 (2). These conditions are imposed by the Act on all schools.

(*m*) **A pupil must not be required.** – See Chapter II, §4, note (*o*). The same provisions apply to a county school.

(*n*) **Inspection of religious instruction given in a county school,** may only be carried out by the persons mentioned, by virtue of S.77 (5). If, in the special circumstances mentioned above in note (*j*), denominational instruction is given to some pupils on the premises of a county secondary school, the Act does not provide for the inspection of such instruction.

# 5. *Secular Instruction in a County School*

Except where otherwise provided in the rules of management or articles of government, the secular instruction in a county school is under the control of the local education authority (*a*). This control includes the power to determine (*b*) the times of the school session, the school terms, holidays, and to require the attendance at classes in secular instruction held off the school premises.

### NOTES
(*a*) **Under the control of the local education authority.** – See S.23 (1) and Chapter II, §5, note (*a*). The same provisions apply to a county school.

(*b*) **Power to determine.** – See S.23 (3) and Chapter II, §5, note (*b*). The same provisions apply to a county school.

# 6. *Teachers in a County School*

The appointment of all teachers in a county school is under the control of the local education authority (*a*), except in so far as such control is delegated to the managers or governors (*b*) under the rules of management or articles of government for the school.

No teacher in a county school may be dismissed except by the authority (*c*).

Other general conditions concerning the appointment and dismissal of teachers in a county school are given below.

### (1) General Conditions applying to all Teachers (*d*)
No person is to be disqualified from being a teacher in a county school by reason of his religious opinions or of his attending or omitting to attend religious worship (*e*). No teacher can be required to give religious instruction (*f*), or receive any less emolument or be deprived of, or disqualified for any promotion or other advantage by reason of the fact that he does or does not give religious instruction, or by reason of his religious opinions, or of his attending or omitting to attend religious worship.

E  cvs

### (2) Women Teachers and Marriage

No woman is to be disqualified for employment as a teacher in a county school, or be dismissed from such employment, by reason only of marriage (*g*).

#### NOTES

(*a*) **Under the control of the local education authority.** – See S.24 (1). All teachers in a county school are employees of the L.E.A.

The L.E.A. may fix the number of teachers to be employed in a school, and, subject to any powers delegated to the managers or governors under the rules of management or articles of government for the school, appoint them.

(*b*) **Except in so far as such control is delegated to the managers or governors.** – See S.24 (1). The articles of government for a county secondary school are made by the L.E.A. and approved by the Secretary of State, who thereby determines, among other things, what measure of the control exercised by the L.E.A. over the appointment of teachers shall be delegated to the governors. The articles, for example, may require the L.E.A. to appoint the head teacher on the recommendation of a joint committee consisting of a number of representatives of the L.E.A. and of an equal number of representatives of the governors. The articles may also require that the assistant teachers in a county secondary school shall be appointed by the governors, subject, possibly, to the right of the L.E.A. to fill a vacancy by transferring a teacher from another school in their area, or from a group of new entrants to the teaching profession appointed by the L.E.A. to their service.

The rules of management for a county primary school are made by the L.E.A., and the L.E.A. may reserve to themselves the power of appointing the teachers.

(*c*) **No teacher in a county school shall be dismissed except by the authority.** – See S.24 (1). The articles of government of a county secondary school, made by the L.E.A. and approved by the Secretary of State, may require the L.E.A. to consult the governors before dismissing a teacher, and may provide that the governors shall be entitled to recommend the dismissal of a teacher. The rules of management for a county primary school are made by the L.E.A., and they may reserve to themselves the right to deal directly with the dismissal of teachers. It should be noted that here, as elsewhere, the education committee or a sub-committee thereof, if the power has been delegated to them by the L.E.A., may act for the authority and deal with the dismissal of teachers.

(*d*) **General conditions relating to all teachers.** – These conditions, popularly described as the 'teachers' charter', are laid down in S.30, and apply to all teachers in a county school. They are to be observed by the L.E.A. and the managers or governors.

(*e*) **Or of his attending or omitting to attend religious worship,** *i.e.* in the school or elsewhere.

(*f*) **No teacher shall be required to give religious instruction.** – By S.25 (2), the L.E.A. are under a statutory obligation to ensure that religious instruction is given in every county school, but the Act gives the individual teacher the freedom to decide for himself, without consequential financial or professional disadvantage, whether he will give religious instruction. It follows that, in practice, a teacher who is to be considered for appointment in a county school should not be asked whether he is prepared to give religious instruction, and that a teacher who is not prepared or able to give agreed syllabus religious instruction should not take up a post – *e.g.* the headship of a one-teacher school – if, by doing so, the L.E.A. would be precluded from fulfilling their statutory obligation – to provide agreed syllabus religious instruction in a county school – by means of the normal establishment of staff for that school.

(*g*) **By reason only of marriage.** – See S.24 (3).

## 7. *Other Employees at a County School*

Any other persons (*a*) employed for the purposes of a county school are to be appointed and dismissed by the authority (*b*). The authority will also determine their conditions of service. No person is to be disqualified for such employment (*c*) by reason of his religious opinions, or of his attending or omitting to attend religious worship.

## NOTES

(*a*) **Any other persons.** – Clerk to the governors, correspondent, clerical staff, school meals staff, caretakers, cleaners, groundsmen. All these employees are employees of the L.E.A.

(*b*) **To be appointed and dismissed by the authority.** – The articles of government or rules of management may provide for the delegation to the governors or managers of the power of appointing or dismissing, or of recommending the appointment or dismissal of, these employees.

Regulations made by the Secretary of State require the L.E.A. to employ staff for their school meals service. The L.E.A. may deal centrally with the appointment and dismissal of such staff, but provision may be made for managers or governors to deal with their appointment and dismissal or of recommending their appointment and dismissal to the L.E.A.

(*c*) **For such employment.** – Disqualification on religious grounds for any of the employments referred to in note (*a*) above, is prohibited by S.30.

# 8. *Maintenance and Use of County School Premises*

The whole cost of maintaining the school premises of a county school falls on the local education authority. The authority control the occupation and use of the premises subject to any powers delegated to the managers or governors under the rules of management or articles of government (*a*).

## NOTE

(*a*) **Under the rules of management or articles of government.** – The rules or articles may delegate powers to the managers or governors with respect to the letting or hiring of the premises, under the regulations of the L.E.A. Any income from such lettings or hirings will be paid over to the L.E.A.

# VI. STATUS AND REORGANIZATION OF SCHOOLS

## 1. *Classification of Existing Schools under the Education Act, 1944*

Primary and secondary schools maintained by a local education authority when the relevant part of the Education Act, 1944, came into operation in 1945, were designated county schools if they had been established by the authority or by a former authority. If they had been established otherwise they were designated voluntary schools. Voluntary schools were divided into three categories: controlled, aided, and special agreement, schools. The status of any particular voluntary school was determined by the Minister, at the instance of its managers or governors, according to their ability and willingness to fulfil the obligations imposed by the Act for the status desired. (*a*)

In the case of other existing schools, such as grammar schools not established by an authority, and assisted, but not maintained, by the authority, their governors were able to apply to the Minister for their school to be maintained by the authority (*b*) under the Education Act, 1944, and their status as aided or controlled schools, was determined by the Minister, at the instance of their governors, according to their ability and willingness to fulfil the obligations imposed by the Act for the status desired.

### NOTES

(*a*) **For the status desired.** – By S.9 (3), existing schools which had been maintained as non-provided public public elementary schools immediately before April 1st, 1945, became voluntary schools on that date. Under S.11, L.E.A.s were required to prepare development plans for their areas. The plans had to specify, amongst other things, the estimated capital cost to be met by the managers or governors in order that their voluntary school premises should comply with the standards prescribed under S.10. After the approval by the Minister of a development plan, managers and governors of existing voluntary schools had to decide whether they were able and willing to defray the expenses which would fall to be borne by them if their school became an aided, or special agreement school, *i.e.* the expenses specified in S.15 (3)*, in respect of the capital expenditure mentioned, and in respect of external repairs to the school buildings. If the managers or governors were unable or unwilling to meet such expenses their school became a controlled school, and the L.E.A. thereupon became responsible for all expenses of maintaining the school. But if, not later than six months after receiving notice of the approval of the development plan for the area, the managers or governors of an existing voluntary school applied to the Minister for an order under S.15 (2) that their school should be an aided school, or a special agreement school, and satisfied him that they were able and willing to defray the expenses mentioned above, with the assistance of the Minister's maintenance contribution, the Minister was required to make an order directing that the school should be an aided school, or, if a special agreement with respect to the school had been made under the Third Schedule to the Act, that the school should be a special agreement school. At the time, the Minister's maintenance contribution, made under S.102*, was 50 per cent.

(*b*) **To be maintained by the authority.** – By submitting a proposal to the Minister under S.13 (2), after consultation with the L.E.A.

68

# 2. *Establishment and Status of a New Voluntary School*

Where it is proposed to establish a new voluntary school, in any of the particular circumstances described in Chapters II, III and IV, a formal proposal must be submitted to the Secretary of State, after consultation with the local education authority (*a*), by the proposers of the new school. Public notice of any such proposal must thereupon be given (*b*). If the proposers desire that the new voluntary school shall be an aided or special agreement school, they must apply to the Secretary of State for the necessary order (*c*), not later than the date on which they submit their proposal (*d*) to establish the new school. If the Secretary of State is satisfied that the proposers are able and willing to meet their share of the cost of providing the new school premises (*e*), and of the subsequent maintenance of the new school buildings (*f*), he is required by the Act to make the order requested (*g*), assuming he approves the establishment of the school.

If the proposers desire that the new voluntary school shall be a controlled school, their application for the necessary order (*c*) has to be made at the time at which they submit their proposal (*h*) for the establishment of the new school.

## NOTES

(*a*) **After consultation with the local education authority.** – See S.13 (2). In the case of a proposed new controlled school, see Chapter II §§ 1 (3) and 1 (4) and the notes thereon for the conditions to be fulfilled.

(*b*) **Public notice must thereupon be given.** – See S.13 (3) as amended by S.16 of the Education (Miscellaneous Provisions) Act, 1953. The notice must be in the form prescribed by the Secretary of State and obtainable from the Department of Education and Science, and must be given in the manner prescribed by the Secretary of State in the *County and Voluntary Schools* (*Notices*) *Regulations, 1945*, as amended by the *County and Voluntary Schools* (*Notices*) *Amending Regulations, 1953*.

(*c*) **Apply to the Secretary of State for the necessary order.** – See S.15 (2).

(*d*) **Not later than the date on which they submit their proposals.** – See the proviso to S.15 (2).

(*e*) **Their share of the cost of providing the new school premises.** – For details see Chapter III, §1, for an aided school and Chapter IV, §2, for a special agreement school.

(*f*) **Maintenance of the new school buildings.** – For details see Chapter III, §8, for an aided school, and Chapter IV, §8, for a special agreement school.

(*g*) **He is required by the Act to make the necessary order.** – By S.15 (2).

(*h*) **At the time at which they submit their proposal.** – See note (*a*) above.

# 3. *Change of Status of a Voluntary School*

A controlled school cannot change its status (*a*) as a voluntary school. If the managers or governors of an aided school or a special agreement school are at any time unable or unwilling to carry out their financial obligations (*b*), they must apply to the Secretary of State for a revocation of the order (*c*) by which their school became an aided school or special agreement school. When such an application is made the Secretary of State must revoke the order and the school will therefore become a controlled school.

A special agreement school may at any time become an aided school (*d*) if the governors repay the grant received by them (*e*) from the local education authority, and if they satisfy the Secretary of State that they are able and willing to meet their share of the cost of any capital expenditure on the school premises and subsequent maintenance of the school buildings. A formal application must be made to the Secretary of State for the revocation of the order by which the school became a special agreement school, and for an order directing that the school shall be an aided school(*f*).

It is always competent for the managers or governors of a voluntary school to make application to the authority for their school to be maintained as a county school. A formal proposal (*g*) must be submitted by the authority to the Secretary of State and a public notice of the proposal (*h*) must be issued. An agreement must also be made (*i*) between the managers or governors and the authority, and be approved by the Secretary of State, for the transfer of all necessary interests in the school premises to the authority.

## NOTES

(*a*) **Cannot change its status.** – No provision for making such a change is included in the Act.

(*b*) **Their financial obligations.** – These are specified in Chapter III and Chapter IV respectively.

(*c*) **Revocation of the order.** – See S.15 (4). Under the Diocesan Education Committee Measures, 1943 and 1955, the managers or governors of a Church of England aided school or special agreement school, who wish to apply to the Secretary of State for a revocation of the order, by which their school became an aided or special agreement school, on the grounds that they are either unwilling or unable to continue to carry out their financial obligations, and accordingly desire that their school shall become a controlled school, are first required to consult their Diocesan Education Committee, and they are also required to consider any representations made to them on the matter by the Diocesan Education Committee. But, having done that, the decision whether to apply to the Secretary of State for the revocation of the order, is one for the managers or governors to make. And the Secretary of State has no option but to revoke the order if so requested.

(*d*) **Become an aided school.** – See S.15 (5).

(*e*) **Repay the grant received by them.** – See §9 of the Third Schedule.

(*f*) **Shall be an aided school.** – See S.15 (5).

(*g*) **A formal proposal,** under S.13 (1) (*b*).

(*h*) **Public notice of the proposal,** under S.13 (3) as amended by S.16 of the Education (Miscellaneous Provisions) Act, 1953.

(*i*) **An agreement must also be made.** – See the proviso to S.13 (4), and the Second Schedule.

## 4. *Reorganization of Schools*

A large number of school mergers will be involved in the reorganization of schools to provide a system of comprehensive schools, simply because it is impossible to discard premises built at considerable cost for a different system of secondary education. The Education Acts, 1944 to 1967, therefore afford considerable flexibility for arranging such mergers (*a*) in suitable circumstances, given the necessary agreements and approvals (*b*).

Any merger must result in the enlargement of one school and the elimination of one or more other schools. The enlargement will almost inevitably involve a proposal and notices under S.13 (*c*), and the elimination will generally be achieved by closure under S.13 (*d*).

The financial arrangements for enlarging the school will depend on its status. If it is a county school, the authority will be responsible for the capital expenditure, and the Secretary of State may direct the authority to meet the cost of the enlargement if the school is a controlled school (e).

Where the enlarged school is an aided or special agreement school, the Secretary of State may pay a grant of 80 per cent of the net expenditure incurred by the managers or governors (f), and may make them a loan to cover the remaining 20 per cent (g).

Where voluntary schools are closed under merger arrangements it will be necessary in some cases for a scheme to be made under the Charities Act, 1960, for the disposal of the endowments or the net sale proceeds of the premises. But there will be other cases in which the existing trusts will make it unnecessary for such a scheme to be made (h).

## NOTES

(a) **Considerable flexibility for arranging such mergers.** – For example of enlargements that may be carried out to provide mergers, see Chapters II, §1 (3), III, §1 (4), and IV, §2 (2), in which the enlarged schools are, respectively, controlled, aided, and special agreement. An example of an enlargement, providing for a merger between a county school and a voluntary school, in which the enlarged school is a county school is given in note (d) below.

(b) **The necessary agreements and approvals,** *i.e.* agreement between the L.E.A. and/or the voluntary bodies concerned, and approvals required by the Secretary of State. It may not be possible to arrange a merger of two voluntary schools where their trusts require them to cater for different denominations.

(c) **Almost inevitably involve a proposal and notices under S.13.** – Because most enlargements for such mergers will provide for an increase of over 25 per cent in the school's recognized accommodation, thereby resulting in a determination under S.67 (4) that the enlargement amounts to the establishment of a new school.

(d) **Will generally be achieved by closure under S.13.** – But the merger of a county school with a voluntary school to result in an enlarged county school may be arranged by a proposal under S.13 (1) (b) for the voluntary school to be maintained as a county school, coupled with a statutory proposal for the school then to be enlarged, to the extent of establishing a new county school, by the addition of the original county school premises. The procedure also involves an agreement between the L.E.A. and the managers or governors of the voluntary school, the agreement to be approved by the Secretary of State, for the transfer of all necessary interests in the premises of the voluntary school to the L.E.A. See the proviso to S.13 (4) and the Second Schedule.

(e) **If the school is a controlled school.** – See note (z) of Chapter II, §1 (3).

(f) **Grant of 80 per cent of the net expenditure incurred by the managers or governors.** – See S.1 (2) (b) of the Education Act, 1967. Also note (t¹) of Chapter III, §1 (4).

(g) **Loan to cover the remaining 20 per cent.** – See S.105 as amended by S.1 (4) of the Education Act, 1967.

(h) **Unnecessary for such a scheme to be made,** *e.g.* if the trust provides that the premises, on ceasing to be used for a school, shall be used for some other purpose; or if the trust provides that the premises, on ceasing to be used for a school, may be claimed by a reversioner, and such a claim is made.

# VII. GENERAL VOLUNTARY SCHOOL PROBLEMS

## 1. *Purchase of Land for Voluntary Schools*

The local education authority have power to purchase land required for a voluntary school, either by agreement (*a*), or compulsorily (*b*). Any part of such land required for voluntary school playing fields will be paid for by the authority and will remain their property. The rest of the land will be conveyed to the trustees of the school, and the cost will be borne by the managers or governors, or by the authority, or partly by both, in accordance with the provisions of the Act (*c*).

### NOTES

(*a*) **By agreement.** – See S.10 (2) of the Education (Miscellaneous Provisions) Act, 1948. This useful provision is to enable the L.E.A. to negotiate on behalf of the managers or governors, and is especially valuable where part or the whole of the purchase money is to be paid by the L.E.A.

(*b*) **Or compulsorily.** – See S.90 as amended by S.10 (1) of the Education (Miscellaneous Provisions) Act, 1948. Managers or governors have no power to acquire land by compulsory purchase, but this provision enables the L.E.A. to act on their behalf.

(*c*) **In accordance with the provisions of the Act.** – The respective responsibilities of the L.E.A. and of the managers or governors of a voluntary school with respect to the provision of a site or an addition to a site are given in detail in Chapters II, III and IV, according to the particular circumstances of each case. See also the proviso to S.90 (1) and S.10 (3) of the Education (Miscellaneous Provisions) Act, 1948.

## 2. *Loans for Aided and Special Agreement Schools*

The Secretary of State has power to make a loan (*a*) to the managers or governors of any aided or special agreement school in respect of their share of any initial expenses required in connection with the school premises, involving capital expenditure, in any of the following cases: (i) on alterations to the school buildings required under the approved development plan, or on alterations to the school buildings which are included in the development plan submitted to the Secretary of State and which are approved by the Secretary of State and carried out before the development plan is approved (*b*); (ii) on the execution of proposals under a special agreement (*c*); (iii) on the transfer of the school to a new site (*d*); (iv) on the establishment of a new school in substitution for a voluntary school or schools to be discontinued (*e*); (v) on the establishment of a new aided school or a new special agreement school, or on the alterations to the school premises of an aided school or special agreement school to the extent of establishing a new school (*f*). Any loan is to be made at the discretion of the Secretary of State, who must be satisfied that the share of capital expenditure to be met by the managers or governors (*g*) ought properly to be met by borrowing (*h*). The amount of the loan, the rate of interest (*i*), and other conditions, such as the period of repayment, are to be specified in an agreement made between the Secretary of State and the managers or governors, with the consent of the Treasury.

## NOTES

(a) **Power to make a loan,** by virtue of S.105 (1). The loan will be in respect of the expenses to be borne by the managers or governors after account has been taken of the Secretary of State's grant to them. If the area served by the aided or special agreement school concerned is a 'single school' area, *i.e.* will not also be served by any county or controlled school, then, before the Secretary of State decides whether to make a loan, he must consult such persons or bodies as appear to him to be representative of any religious denomination which, in his opinion, having regard to the circumstances of the area, is likely to be concerned; and unless, after such consultation, the Secretary of State is satisfied that the holding of a local inquiry is unnecessary, he must cause such inquiry to be held (see S.93) before deciding whether to make a loan. See S.105 (3).

(b) **On alterations to the school buildings** included in the approved development plan, by virtue of S.105 (2) (a); on alterations included in the development plan submitted to the Secretary of State which are approved by the Secretary of State and carried out before the approval of the development plan, by virtue of S.105 (2) (a) as amended by S.8 (3) (a) of the Education (Miscellaneous Provisions) Act, 1953.

(c) **On the execution of proposals under a special agreement,** by virtue of S.105 (2) (b).

(d) **On the transfer of the school to a new site,** *i.e.* in providing the school buildings, whether by the erection of new buildings or by the purchase of existing buildings, or by the purchase and adaptation of existing buildings, by virtue of S.105 (2) (c) as amended by S.8 (3) (b) (i) of the Education (Miscellaneous Provisions) Act, 1953.

(e) **On the establishment of a new school in substitution for a voluntary school or schools to be discontinued,** *i.e.* in providing the site for the new school and in providing the school buildings, whether by purchase of existing premises, or by the purchase and adaptation of existing premises, or by the erection of new buildings on a site acquired for that purpose, by virtue of S.105 (2) (c) as amended by S.8 (3) (b) (ii) of the Education (Miscellaneous Provisions) Act, 1953.

(f) **On the establishment of a new aided school or a new special agreement school,** *i.e.* in providing the site for the new school and in providing the school buildings, whether by the purchase of existing premises, or by the purchase and adaptation of existing premises, or by the erection of new buildings on a site acquired for that purpose, by virtue of S.1 (4) of the Education Act, 1967, which includes such expenses in the expression 'initial expenses' of S.105.

(g) **Share of the capital expenditure to be met by the managers or governors,** *i.e.* after taking account of the Secretary of State's grant to them.

(h) **Ought properly to be met by borrowing.** – See S.105 (1). The Secretary of State is to be the sole judge of this point. No application for a loan of less than £500 will be entertained.

(i) **Rate of interest.** – Managers or governors are advised of the current rate of interest at the time of the inclusion of their project in the building programme, or on the approval in principle of the project. The Treasury vary the interest rate from time to time, but the change, which is publicly announced, affects only loans or instalments of loans drawn after the operative date of the change.

# 3. *Boarding Accommodation at Voluntary Schools*

Boarding accommodation provided as part of a school (a), whether in the main or detached buildings, forms part of the school premises (b). In the case of a controlled school, the local education authority must meet the cost of maintaining the boarding-house. In the case of an aided or special agreement school, the responsibilities for the maintenance of the boarding-house rest between the local education authority and the managers or governors in precisely the same way as the maintenance of the school (c).

If accommodation is provided within the boarding-house for the housemaster or house tutor, that accommodation is part of the school premises (d). If a separate house is provided (e) for the housemaster or house tutor for his occupation as such, it is not a teacher's dwelling-house, but is part of the school premises.

## NOTES

(a) **Provided as part of a school,** *i.e.* in the case of a voluntary school, if the boarding accommodation has been provided under the trust deed or scheme governing the foundation, or, otherwise, if the managers or governors of an aided or special agreement school provide a boarding-house, or if the L.E.A. provide a boarding-house for a controlled school.

(b) **Forms part of the school premises,** because it is not excluded from the definition of premises in S.114 (1)*. The boarding-house is also a school building (see Chapter I, §2) by virtue of *S.4 (2)*.

(c) **Same way as the maintenance of the school,** *i.e.* running costs to be met by the L.E.A., external repairs by the managers or governors, in the case of an aided or special agreement school (with the 80 per cent maintenance contribution from the Secretary of State) and by the L.E.A. for a controlled school; internal repairs by the L.E.A. in all cases. As regards any capital expenditure, the responsibilities of the managers or governors, and the L.E.A., and grants by the Secretary of State to managers and governors of aided and special agreement schools, are precisely the same as in the corresponding case of the usual school buildings.

(d) **Accommodation within the boarding-house is part of the school premises,** thereby involving the L.E.A. for the cost of the whole of its maintenance, in the case of a controlled school, and for the running costs and internal repairs in the case of an aided or special agreement school.

(e) **If a separate house is provided for the housemaster or house tutor.** – By S.114 (1)* a teacher's dwelling-house does not form part of the school premises. The question whether a house provided for the housemaster of a school boarding-house was a teacher's dwelling-house or whether it was part of the school premises was determined by the Lands Tribunal in 1951 in *Brice and Ward v. Hampshire County Council* appeal case. The question was whether the housemaster's house at a voluntary school was a teacher's dwelling-house, within the meaning of S.114 (1)* and, therefore, subject to the payment of rates, or whether it was part of the voluntary school premises, and, therefore, under S.64, exempt from rates (that is to say, before the Rating and Valuation Act, 1961). The Lands Tribunal decided that the dwelling was an essential part of the boarding-house, and was occupied by the master so that he could be in a position out of school hours to supervise the boarding pupils and, accordingly, was not a teacher's dwelling-house but was part of the school premises.

It follows that rent is not chargeable to the housemaster for the house, or to the L.E.A., and that, in the case of a controlled school, the L.E.A. are responsible for all improvements to the house, and for all internal and external repairs and decorations. And that, in the case of an aided or special agreement school, the managers or governor are responsible for all improvements and for external repairs and decoration, towards which the Secretary of State will pay a grant of 80 per cent, and the L.E.A. are responsible for all internal repairs and decorations of the house.

Under the Rating and Valuation Act, 1961, rates will become payable on the house – see Chapter II, §8, note (h), which applies equally to controlled, aided and special agreement schools – and the L.E.A. will be responsible for the payment of the rates on the house.

## 4. *Teacher's Dwelling-house*

A teacher's dwelling-house does not form part of the school premises (a). There is, however, nothing to prevent a local education authority from providing such a house for a teacher who is employed by them (b). A teacher's dwelling-house which is provided by the trustees of a voluntary school is their property: the relationship between them and the teacher is a matter for them to determine (c), and neither the authority nor the Secretary of State have any obligations in the matter (d).

## NOTES

(*a*) **Does not form part of the school premises,** by virtue of the definition of 'school premises' in S.114 (1)\*. See also Chapter I, §2, note (*b*). See also Chapter VII, §3, note (*e*).

(*b*) **For a teacher who is employed by them,** *i.e.* a teacher in a county, controlled or special agreement school.

(*c*) **Is a matter for them to determine,** under the agreement made with the teacher on appointment.

(*d*) **Any obligations in the matter.** – The L.E.A. may arrange for a lease of the teacher's dwelling-house from the trustees of a controlled or special agreement school; and, in the event of an arrangement under the Second Schedule for the transfer of an interest in the premises of any voluntary school to the L.E.A. for the purpose of enabling the L.E.A. to maintain the school as a county school, the teacher's dwelling-house may be included in the transfer of that interest.

## 5. *Privately-owned Controlled Schools*

Privately-owned controlled schools present a special problem for the local education authority. In the first place, when such a voluntary school became a controlled school, the local education authority became liable to meet the rent (*a*). In most cases the rent charged by the owner when the school was a non-provided school was a nominal one, and might remain so; but, except where otherwise provided in the lease of the premises to the managers or governors, the owner may vary the rent, and, indeed, if the managers or governors of such a school had obtained a long lease of the premises at a rack-rent, the local education authority will have to meet that rent under that lease. If a proposal is made to vary the rent of a privately-owned school after it has become a controlled school, the local education authority should take up the question, in case it is to their advantage to acquire the premises (*b*), and to retain the ownership of the property (*c*). In many cases, and whether the rent is nominal or not, it is desirable to do so, because the local education authority may have to undertake substantial repairs, for which they are responsible (*d*), and to carry out necessary improvements (*e*) before there is any prospect of discontinuing the school, or of altering the premises, or of transferring the school to a new site, according to the proposed future of the school. In any event, if it is proposed to alter the premises then before the alteration is carried out by the local education authority (*f*), the authority will normally wish to acquire the original premises (*g*). If it is proposed to transfer the school to a new site, the local education authority will have to provide (*h*) the new site and any buildings on it which are to form part of the school premises and convey their interests in the new site and such buildings to the trustees of the school (*i*). The local education authority will have to provide the playing fields (*j*) and any buildings required for use in connection therewith, but will retain them as their property (*k*). If the old school premises are still privately owned at that time, they will remain the property of the owner. If they have been acquired by the local education authority the authority may then dispose of the old premises.

## NOTES

(*a*) **Meet the rent.** – The L.E.A. must meet the rent by virtue of S.114 (2) and S.15 (3)\*.

(*b*) **To acquire the premises.** – By compulsory purchase, if necessary, under S.90, or by agreement under S.10 (2) of the Education (Miscellaneous Provisions) Act, 1948.

(c) **Retain the ownership of the property.** – The L.E.A. are under no obligation to convey the premises to trustees. The L.E.A. have no power to require that a privately-owned voluntary school shall become a county school on their purchase of the premises.

(d) **For which they are responsible.** – See S.114 (2) and S.15 (3)*.

(e) **Necessary improvements.** – Most privately-owned controlled schools need improvements, of a sort that can be carried out before discontinuance, or major alteration, etc., and their cost may be substantial; and the L.E.A. will be disinclined to improve private property.

(f) **Carried out by the local education authority.** – The duty of the L.E.A. to maintain a controlled school is defined in S.114 (2), and includes all expenditure on alterations by virtue of that definition and S.15 (3)*.

(g) **Authority will acquire the original premises,** which will then remain their property, but if the alterations required by the development plan involve an addition to the site and the erection of buildings thereon, then, although *S.3* and *§1 of the First Schedule* require the L.E.A. to meet the cost, they must by *S.3* and *§6 of the First Schedule* convey their interests in the addition to the site and the buildings thereon to trustees, with the safeguard provided by *§8 of the First Schedule*.

(h) **Local education authority will have to provide.** – The L.E.A. must meet the cost by virtue of *S.3* and *§1 of the First Schedule*. See Chapter II, §1, for the conditions under which a controlled school may be transferred to a new site.

(i) **Trustees of the school.** – See *S.3* and *§6 of the First Schedule*. See also *§8 of the First Schedule*.

(j) **Playing fields.** – See Chapter II, §1, note (e).

(k) **Will retain them as their property.** – See Chapter II, §1, note (m).

# 6. *Fire Insurance of Controlled Schools*

If the premises of a controlled school are damaged or destroyed by fire, the duty to repair or replace them (a) falls on the local education authority. The authority will therefore insure against their risks and no responsibility for such insurance (b) rests on the managers or governors or trustees. The insurance to be effected is for the whole of the school premises (c). The teacher's house (d) is excluded from the school premises, and, unless the local education authority have provided the house for their employee, or have leased such a house from the trustees of the school, they have no power to insure it: the insurance of such a house provided at the school by the trustees or private owner is a matter for them.

In order to secure the favourable insurance terms available to a public body, the local education authority will make the arrangements for the insurance of the premises of controlled schools against fire, rather than meet the premiums (e) on insurances arranged by the managers, governors, or trustees. The insurance policy should safeguard the reversionary interests of the trustees, and the local education authority should give them the necessary assurances, in the policy, or otherwise.

It is desirable that the insurance cover shall take into account all the expenses that the authority will have to incur if the premises have to be replaced after destruction by fire.

If the premises of a controlled school are destroyed by fire, the capital sum payable by the insurance company, under the arrangements mentioned above, will be received by the local education authority, with a due safeguard of the reversionary interests of the trustees. If the premises are rebuilt or if they are replaced by premises which conform to the larger requirements of the Education Act, 1944, the local education authority will have to meet the cost. In either case, if the old premises belonged to trustees, the local education authority will have to convey the new premises to them and will retain the capital sum received from the insurance company.

In the case of a privately-owned controlled school, the arrangements for fire insurance of the premises will depend on the terms of the lease or tenancy of the premises.

Arrangements for the insurance of the premises against damage by aircraft follow those described above for insurance against fire.

### NOTES

(a) **The duty to repair or replace them** falls on the L.E.A. by S.114 (2) and S.15 (3)*.

(b) **No responsibility for such insurance** rests on the managers, governors or trustees by virtue of S.15 (3)* and S.114 (2). Where the premises are privately-owned, the arrangements for fire insurance will be made in the terms of the lease approved by the L.E.A.

(c) **Whole of the school premises.** – Previously, parts of the buildings required only for the provision of milk, meals, and other refreshment for pupils were not insured as their repair or replacement was met in full by the Secretary of State's grant. Under S.14 of the Local Government Act, 1966, that no longer obtains from April 1st, 1967.

(d) **The teacher's house.** – See Chapter VII, §4.

(e) **Meet the premiums.** – The L.E.A. must meet the premiums in any case by S.114 (2), subject to what is mentioned in note (b) above, in the case of a privately-owned school.

## 7. Fire Insurance of Aided and Special Agreement Schools

The local education authority are responsible for the following repairs at aided and special agreement schools, and therefore for the corresponding repair or replacement after fire: (i) repairs to the interior of the school buildings (a), (ii) all repairs to the rest of the premises. The managers or governors are responsible (b) for repairs to the school buildings other than repairs to the interior of such buildings, and are therefore responsible for the corresponding repairs or replacement after fire.

In view of the divided responsibility for repairs or replacement, there is divided responsibility for insurance against fire. Each party may insure against its separate risks, but such an arrangement is administratively inconvenient, and a joint insurance (c) has much to commend it. Such a joint insurance should be effected by the managers, governors, trustees, or, preferably, on their behalf, by the competent diocesan or central church authority (d). An assessment of the respective responsibilities (e) of the two parties has to be made, whether a joint insurance or separate insurances are arranged.

The teacher's house (f) is excluded from the school premises, and unless, in the case of a special agreement school, the local education authority have provided a house for their employee, or have leased such a house from the trustees of the school, they have no power to insure it: the insurance of such a house provided at the school by the trustees or private owner is a matter for them.

Assuming that a joint insurance of the premises has been arranged by the voluntary body, if the premises are destroyed by fire, the capital sum will be payable to the trustees, with a due safeguard of the interests of the local education authority. If the premises are rebuilt, both the trustees and the local education authority will be involved in expenditure, and will be entitled to their respective shares of the capital sum paid by the insurance company. The new premises (g) will be the property of the trustees. If the old premises did not conform to the requirements of the Education Act, 1944, and the new premises are to meet these requirements, each party will have to meet its share of the expenditure attributable to replacement of the old premises and will receive its share of the capital sum paid by the insurance company towards it; but, as regards the new provision to be made in excess of mere replacement of the old premises, the managers and governors will be responsible for the whole of the expenditure on the school buildings (h), and the local education authority for the expenditure on other buildings (i).

If the premises of the aided or special agreement school are privately owned, the arrangements for the fire insurance of the premises will depend on the terms of the lease or tenancy, and, having regard to the position described above in the general case, the local education authority will safeguard their position accordingly.

Arrangements for insurance against damage by aircraft follow the arrangements described above.

### NOTES

(a) **Repairs to the interior of the school buildings.** – These are the responsibility of the L.E.A. by virtue of S.15 (3)*. School buildings are defined in Chapter I, §2, and what constitutes repairs to the interior of school buildings is explained in Chapter VII, §10. The L.E.A. are responsible for all repairs to the other buildings (see Chapter I, §2).

(b) **The managers or governors are responsible** for repairs to the school buildings, other than repairs to the interior of such buildings, by virtue of S.15 (3)*. Arrangements should be made to cover the use of the premises by the L.E.A. under S.22 (2), when they are not required for the purposes of the school.

(c) **Joint insurance.** – Separate insurance arrangements may involve two insurance companies dealing with two claims by different parties in respect of one fire, and over-lapping or omission of cover.

(d) **Diocesan or Central Church Authority.** – Such bodies can obtain the same favourable insurance terms as a public body, and are accustomed to deal with insur-ances on behalf of managers. The possibility of an insurance policy dealing with all the aided and special agreement schools of a given denomination in the area of the L.E.A. is envisaged here. Agreement may be reached for the L.E.A. to make the insurance arrangements on behalf of both parties, but the diocesan authority will normally have dealt with the insurance of voluntary school premises and other denominational property, and the L.E.A. will not wish to disturb such arrangements unnecessarily. In the case of a privately-owned school, it may be possible to bring it under joint insurance arrangements with the diocesan authority.

(e) **Assessment of the respective responsibilities.** – To do this precisely would involve an analysis equivalent to that of a bill of quantities. A precise apportionment in each individual case would depend on the type of the premises, e.g. single-storey, double-storey, and so on, and on the precise division between school buildings and other buildings. In practice, particularly where insurance arrangements have been made on a diocesan basis with the L.E.A., agreement has been reached that external repairs or replacement (the responsibility of the managers or governors) shall be regarded as accounting for half the total, and internal repairs or replacement (the responsibility of the L.E.A.) as accounting for the other half – but see note (i) below. As to the amount of premiums payable under such arrangements, it must be remembered that under the Local Government Act, 1966, the L.E.A. receive no specific exchequer grant towards their expenditure on repair or replacement after a fire. But, as regards the expenditure on repair or replacement to be met by the managers or governors, the Secretary of State has to meet 80 per cent of the cost under the Education Act, 1967. The amount of the fire insurance premium payable by the managers or governors is therefore small. The Secretary of State will not make a maintenance contribution towards the premiums payable by the managers or governors, but, as mentioned, he will meet 80 per cent of the approved costs attributable to external repairs or replacement.

(*f*) **The teacher's house.** – See Chapter VII, §4.

(*g*) **The new premises** will be the property of the trustees or private owners, with the exception of the playing fields and any buildings on them for use in connection therewith, provided by the L.E.A., which remain the property of the L.E.A.

(*h*) **Whole of the expenditure on the school buildings,** *i.e.* for the school buildings which are new and not in replacement of the destroyed school buildings. But if this alteration of the premises amounts to the establishment of a new school – see S.67 (4) – and is approved by the Secretary of State – see S.1 (2) (*b*) of the Education Act, 1967, they will receive a grant of 80 per cent of their approved expenditure thereon from the Secretary of State. If the alteration does not amount to the establishment of a new school, the approved expenditure of the managers or governors thereon will be eligible for a maintenance contribution of 80 per cent from the Secretary of State under S.102, as amended by the Education Act, 1946, and by S.1 (1) of the Education Act, 1967.

(*i*) **For the other half.** – That arrangement was commonly made when the parts of the buildings required only for the provision of milk, meals, and other refreshment for pupils were not insured – see note (*c*) of §6 above which applies equally to aided and special agreement schools. From April 1st, 1967, the additional insurance involved is the responsibility of the L.E.A.

# 8. *Other Insurances at Voluntary Schools*

## (1) Negligence of Employees

All persons employed at controlled or special agreement schools are employees of the local education authority. If accidents occur as a result of their negligence when they are acting within the scope of their employment (*a*), the authority will be liable. Any question of insurance against such legal liabilities is therefore a matter for the local education authority, not for the managers or governors. In an aided school, the position is exactly the same, as that described above, as regards persons employed in the school meals service, because they are employees of the authority (*b*). All other employees at an aided school are employees of the managers or governors, so that a liability for accidents occurring as a result of their negligence, if they are acting within the scope of their employment (*a*), may attach to the managers or governors. But the authority are responsible for maintaining the school, including the payment of the salaries of those servants, and they are also concerned with the control of the secular instruction. The authority, therefore, will generally be responsible for meeting the costs (*c*) of successful claims against the managers or governors arising from the negligence of employees at an aided school, acting within the scope of their employment.

If persons are employed by the managers or governors of any controlled, aided, or special agreement school, in connection with the use of the premises by them, or by any bodies to whom the managers or governors may let or hire the premises out of school hours, the managers or governors will be liable for accidents occurring as a result of the negligence of their servants acting within the scope of their employment.

Managers and governors will insure against such risks, and, in the case of denominational schools, will be able to do so more cheaply by making their arrangements through the diocesan authority. Payment of the premiums will not be recognized by the Secretary of State for his maintenance contribution (d).

### (2) Defects in the Premises

Managers and governors of voluntary schools are the occupiers of the school premises. As such, they owe a duty, at common law, of care to persons on the premises. If, therefore, accidents occur as a result of a defect in the premises, the managers or governors will normally be made the defendants in any legal action, even though the local education authority may be joined as co-defendants.

The authority are responsible in such cases if the accident is attributable to a defect which they are under a statutory duty to remedy (e). In the case of a controlled school, therefore, the duty of the local education authority to maintain the premises may give complete protection to the managers or governors, but everything depends on the circumstances of the particular case. In practice, the authority will usually cover the managers and governors of controlled schools, except as regards insurance against their common law risks when the premises are used out of school hours by the managers or governors, or by any bodies to whom they have let or hired the premises. Against this risk, managers and governors of denominational controlled schools will be able to get cheaper insurance terms through their diocesan authority (f).

In the case of aided and special agreement schools, managers and governors will insure against their common law risks in respects of accidents from defects in the premises which they are under a duty to remedy (g). The payment of such insurance premiums will not be eligible for the Secretary of State's maintenance contribution; and similarly, as regards their insurance against their common law risks for the use of the premises out of school hours by them, or by bodies to whom they let or hire the premises.

### (3) Employees

In view of the provisions of the National Insurance Acts, the local education authority will only consider insuring against their common law risks as regards employees at schools.

Managers and governors will insure against such risks so far as they are concerned both as regards the use of the school premises during and after school hours.

### NOTES

(a) **Within the scope of their employment.** – Employees may sometimes act outside the scope of their employment, in which case the L.E.A. are not liable, *e.g. Dixon v. Roper, The Times,* February 3rd, 1922, in which a matron gave a birthday present to a schoolboy, resulting in an accident.

(b) **Are employees of the authority.** – Under the *Provision of Milk and Meals Regulations, 1945.*

(c) **For meeting the costs.** – The L.E.A. are responsible for maintaining the school, and if the circumstances are incidental, to that, the L.E.A. will be liable to meet the costs. In a Workmen's Compensation case in 1907 (*Justice of the Peace,* Vol. 71, p. 329) the Board of Education gave their opinion that a payment of Workmen's Compensation was a necessary incident of running a school. If the managers of a voluntary school had to pay damages through being vicariously liable for the negligence of their employee, that might well be regarded as an expense of maintaining the school.

(*d*) **Not be recognized for the Secretary of State's maintenance contributions.** – It is not included in S.102 as expenditure that the Secretary of State can so recognize for grant.

(*e*) **Which they are under a statutory duty to remedy.** – In the case of controlled schools the L.E.A. are responsible for all expenses of maintaining the premises. In an aided or special agreement school, the L.E.A. are responsible for repairs to the interior of the school buildings, and for external and internal repairs to other buildings.

Rules of management and articles of government commonly require the managers or governors to inspect the premises and to keep the L.E.A. informed as to the state of repair of the premises. In the case of neglect to inspect there may be a liability on the managers or governors, but the L.E.A. should cover them against that, in so far as the remedying of the defects are the duty of the L.E.A.

(*f*) **Through their diocesan authority,** who, dealing with many schools, can obtain more favourable insurance terms than a single body of managers or governors.

(*g*) **Which they are under a duty to remedy.** – Namely, defects arising through failure to do external repairs to the school buildings, which are the responsibility of the managers or governors. Note also the case of *Abbott v. Isham* (1921) in which the managers of a non-provided school were held liable for the injury caused to the headmaster through the bursting of the school boiler, about which he had complained on many occasions since 1905. The managers were held to be liable because it was their duty to take reasonable care to provide proper appliances and to maintain them in a proper condition so as not to subject those employed by them to unnecessary risk.

# 9. *Furniture, Equipment, and Fittings in Aided and Special Agreement Schools*

(1) The original provision of all furniture, equipment, and fittings in the other buildings (*a*) of aided and special agreement schools, is the responsibility of the local education authority.

(2) The original provision of all furniture and equipment, and some fittings in the school buildings (*b*) of aided and special agreement schools, is the responsibility of the local education authority.

(3) The repair or replacement of all furniture, all equipment, and all fittings (*c*), both in the school buildings and other buildings of aided and special agreement schools, is the responsibility of the local education authority.

(4) The managers or governors of aided and special agreement schools are responsible for the original provision of the following fittings in new school buildings, and in alterations or extensions of school buildings, in order to meet their obligations under the *Standards for School Premises Regulations, 1959*, and towards which they are eligible to receive 80 per cent of their approved expenditure from the Secretary of State.

(i) *Assembly Hall:* Fixed stage, permanent proscenium, general lighting of hall and stage, and power points for theatrical lighting.

(ii) *Lighting Fittings:* Electric wiring, fittings, globes, bulbs.

(iii) *Heating Fittings:* Radiators, gas fires, electric fires, fire-places, stoves.

F cvs

(iv) *Cloak Rooms:* Coat pegs, store racks, in cloak rooms and drying rooms.

(v) *Storerooms:* Racks and shelves.

(vi) *Sanitary Fittings:* Wash bowls, sanitary sinks, water closets, urinals, flushing cisterns, shower baths, slipper baths, water heating systems.

(vii) *Various Services:* Electric wiring and power points, water, and gas pipes, to points specified by the local education authority throughout the school buildings, including, particularly, science rooms, handicraft rooms, and domestic science rooms.

(5) If, in the provision of new school buildings, or the alteration or extension of school buildings, any fixed furniture, equipment, and such fittings as are the responsibility of the local education authority, are to be included in the building contract of the managers or governors, it is a matter for the local education authority to specify the items during the preparation of the plans, and, if need be, during the progress of the contract. The list of such items may be large, but, having regard to the items for which the managers and governors are responsible, set out above, the division of responsibility is clear. For such items as are specified by the local education authority to be included in the building contract of the managers or governors, and for which the local education authority are to accept responsibility, that responsibility will also include the cost of supplying and fixing, and a proportion of preliminaries, fees, clerk of work's salary, and incidental expenses.

### NOTES

(a) **Other buildings.** – See Chapter I, §2.

(b) **School buildings.** – See Chapter I, §2. The fittings for which the L.E.A. are responsible are those which do not come within the list set out above in §9 (4) as being those for which the managers or governors are responsible.

(c) **Repair or replacement.** – Under S.15 (3)*, the L.E.A. are responsible for all internal repairs.

## 10. *Responsibility for Repairs to the Premises of Aided and Special Agreement Schools*

The local education authority are responsible for all repairs to the premises of aided and special agreement schools, except to the school buildings (a). There the responsibility is divided: the authority are responsible for repairs to the interior of the school buildings (b), and the managers or governors are responsible for the other repairs to the school buildings (c). It is therefore of considerable practical importance to the local education authority and to the managers or governors to know what is meant by the phrase 'repairs to the interior of the school buildings'. The term 'school buildings' is precisely defined in the Act, but there is no statutory definition of 'repairs to the interior' of the school buildings.

In the last resort what are and what are not repairs to the interior of school buildings of aided and special agreement schools can only be settled by the Courts.

The schedule and accompanying diagram given at the end of this chapter, separate the various items according to the respective responsibilities of the local education authority and the managers and governors for repairs to the school buildings.

We have made our analysis by reference to the available authorities (*d*) dealing with the construction of a covenant to do internal or external repairs as between landlord and tenant.

It must be borne in mind that the schedule and diagram refer only to the school buildings, and that the local education authority are responsible for all repairs to the other buildings (*e*), and for all repairs to the rest of the school premises, including the school grounds.

Repairs for which the managers or governors are responsible are eligible for the Secretary of State's maintenance contribution (*f*).

## NOTES

(*a*) **School buildings** are defined in *S.4* (2) as any building or part of any building forming part of the school premises, except that it does not include any building or part of a building required **only** (i) as a caretaker's dwelling; (ii) for use in connection with playing fields; (iii) for affording facilities for enabling the local education authority to carry out their functions with respect to medical inspection or treatment; or (iv) for affording facilities for providing milk, meals or other refreshment for pupils in attendance at the school.

(*b*) **Repairs to the interior of the school buildings** are the responsibility of the L.E.A. by S.15 (3) (*b*)*.

(*c*) **Other repairs to the school buildings** are the responsibility of the managers or governors by S.15 (3) (*a*)*.

(*d*) **Available authorities.** – In *Green v. Eales* ([1841] 2 Q.B. 225) the 'external parts of the premises' are defined as 'those which form the inclosure of them and beyond which no part of them extends, and it is immaterial whether these parts are exposed to the atmosphere, or rest upon and adjoin some other building which forms no part of the premises let'. The definition was quoted with approval in 1940 in *Pembery v. Lamdia*. Stroud's *Judicial Dictionary* also states that the phrase 'external parts' includes the windows, they being part of the skin of the house.

Again, in *Howe v. Botwood* ([1913] K.B. 387) it was held, in dealing with the liability to do external repairs, that the covenant imposed on the covenantor, the liability to repair the drainage system outside the house, even though the work involved reconstruction required by the local authority under the Public Health Acts.

(*e*) **Repairs to the other buildings,** *i.e.* to all buildings which are not school buildings. It should be noted that in this paragraph only the question of repairs is considered. As regards alterations, improvements, and the provision of new buildings, reference should be made to the appropriate chapter dealing with the particular kind of school.

(*f*) **Secretary of State's maintenance contribution.** – See S.102 as amended by S.1 (1) of the Education Act, 1967. The Secretary of State will pay 80 per cent of the approved cost of repairs met by the managers or governors.

RESPONSIBILITY FOR REPAIRS TO SCHOOL BUILDINGS OF AIDED AND SPECIAL AGREEMENT SCHOOLS

| Item | Responsibility of Managers or Governors | Responsibility of L.E.A. |
|---|---|---|
| Roof (wood-framed) | Slates or Tiles; Boards; Laths; Sarking; Ridge; Purlins; Barge Boards; Gutters, Boards and Bearers; Snowboards; Wall Plate; Roof Lights; Flashings | Roof Trusses |
| Roof (concrete) | Roof Covering; Skirtings; Concrete Slab; Beams; Fillets; Kerbs; Roof Lights; Flashings | |
| Ceiling | | Internal Finish, if Plaster or similar |
| | | Joists; Bearers; Plaster and/or Boards; Gangway; Hatches; and all repairs |
| External Walls | Foundation; Damp Proof Course; Walling (full width); Pointing; Ventilators; Heads; Arches; Lintels; Sills; Steps; Flues above Roof Level; Roughcast; Corbels supporting Roof Trusses | Internal Plaster, Tiles or similar finish (excluding a finish which is an integral part of the wall, i.e. glazed brick); Skirting; Picture Rail; Cover Moulds; Chimney Breasts; Fireplaces; Boundary Walls and Fencing |
| Floors | | All repairs, including Sub-Floor, Sleeper Walls, Fender Walls, Wall Plate |
| Internal Division Walls | | Foundations; Damp Proof Course; Spandril Walls; Walling to Roof Level; Chimney Breasts and Flues to Roof Level; Plaster or other finish; and all repairs |
| External Doors | Doors; Frames; Locks; Hinges; Furniture; Glass; External Moulds | Internal Architraves; Linings and Cover Moulds in relation thereto |
| Windows | Frames; Sashes; Sills; Glass; External Moulds; Pulleys; Hinges | Sash Cords; Opening Cords; Casement Stays; Slide Cheeks; Pulls and Fasteners; Window Boards; Linings; Cover Moulds; Internal Architraves; Internal Screens |
| Internal Doors | | All repairs |
| Drainage | All External Drainage; Gullies; Manholes; Soil and Vent Pipes | All Internal Waste or Drains |
| Plumbing | All Gas and Water Services outside building; External Rain-water Pipes; All Gutters; Flashings and Soakers; External Drinking Fountains; Wastes, Drains and Overflows | Inside Rainwater Pipes; W.C. Suites; Lavatory Basins and Fittings; Internal Drinking Fountains; Internal Traps; Wastes; All Internal Plumbing and Fitting |
| Electrical Work | External Service Cables; Outside Lights | All Internal Cables and Fittings |
| Heating | | All Heating Apparatus and Fittings of all types |
| Painting and Decoration | External | Internal |

NOTE. – The line of demarcation between External and Internal is taken to mean the line on the inside face of an outer wall; e.g. a plaster finish on the inside of an outer wall is internal.

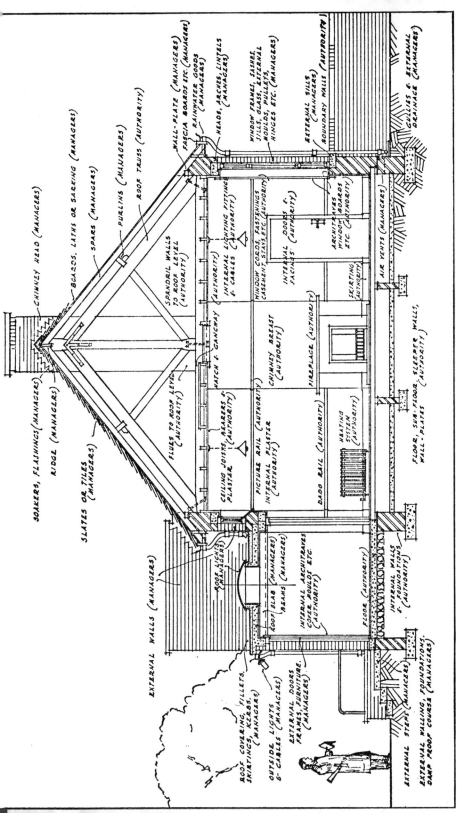

# APPENDICES

## Specimen Instruments and Rules of Management and Instruments and Articles of Government of Voluntary Schools

The Instrument of Management of a primary school and the Instrument of Government of a secondary school deal with the constitution and method of appointment of the body of managers or governors and regulate their meetings and proceedings. The following specimen instrument of management may be read, subject to the variations mentioned, as an instrument of management of a controlled or of an aided primary school, or, if 'governors' is substituted for 'managers', and 'clerk to the governors' for 'correspondent to the managers', etc., as an instrument of government of a controlled, a special agreement, or an aided, secondary school.

In the case of a middle school, S.1(2) of the Education Act, 1964, provides that the Secretary of State shall direct whether it shall be deemed to be a primary school or a secondary school for the purposes of the Education Acts. The Secretary of State will be prepared to consider the preference expressed by the L.E.A.

In the following specimen instruments, rules, and articles, no attempt has been made to deal with the special variations required in the case of schools that are administered indirectly by a local education authority through a divisional executive, as the delegation of functions from an authority to a divisional executive depends on the particular scheme of divisional administration. But for any given scheme of divisional administration, the necessary amendments to the specimen instruments, rules, or articles, given here, can be made quite simply by reference to the actual terms of the scheme.

## I. Specimen Instrument of Management

### Interpretations

1. In this Instrument, unless the context otherwise requires, the following expressions shall have the meanings hereby assigned to them:

'The Act' means the Education Act, 1944, as amended by any subsequent enactment;

'The Local Education Authority' means the County Council of the Administrative County (a) of X. and, where a function has been delegated to a Committee of the County Council or to any Sub-Committee of such a Committee, includes in relation to such function the Committee or Sub-Committee to whom the exercise of such function is delegated.

'Secretary of State' means the Secretary of State for Education and Science.

Other expressions to which meanings are assigned by the Act shall have the same meanings as are assigned to them in the Act.

The Interpretation Act, 1889, shall apply to the interpretation of this Instrument as it applies to an Act of Parliament.

### Body of Managers

2. The body of Managers of the A.B. Primary School (hereinafter called 'the school'), shall, when complete, consist of:

[For typical illustrations of different constitutions of managing and governing bodies according to the classification and character of the schools, see particulars at the end of this specimen instrument.]

86

## Term of Office

3. Every Manager to be appointed by the local education authority shall be appointed for a term of office ending on the date of the appointment of his successor, which may be made at any time after the ordinary day of retirement of County Councillors next after his appointment. The other Managers, other than the *ex-officio* Manager (*b*), shall be appointed each for a term of three years (*c*).

## First Managers and Meeting

4. (i) The first Managers, other than an *ex-officio* Manager (*b*), shall be appointed as soon as possible after the date of this Instrument and their names shall be notified to the Correspondent to the existing body of Managers (*d*).

(ii) The first meeting of the Managers under this Instrument shall be summoned by the said Correspondent (*e*) as soon as conveniently may be after the date of this Instrument, or if he fails to summon a meeting for two months after that date by any two Managers.

## Managers not to be financially interested in the School

5. Except in special circumstances (*f*) with the approval in writing of the Secretary of State, no Manager shall take or hold any interest in any property held or used for the purposes of the school, otherwise than as a trustee for the purposes thereof, or receive any remuneration for his services (*g*), or be interested in the supply of work or goods to or for the purposes of the school.

## Determination of Managership

6. Any Manager, other than an *ex-officio* Manager (*h*), who is absent from all meetings of the Managers during a period of one year, and any Manager who is adjudicated a bankrupt, or who is incapacitated from acting, or who communicates in writing to the Correspondent to the Managers a wish to resign, shall thereupon cease to be a Manager.

## Vacancies

7. Every vacancy in the office of Manager, other than an *ex-officio* Manager, shall as soon as possible be notified to the proper appointing body, and any competent Manager may be reappointed.

## Casual Vacancies

8. A Manager appointed to fill a casual vacancy shall hold office only for the unexpired term of office of the Manager in whose place he is appointed.

## Employees not to be Managers

9. No master or other person employed for the purposes of the school shall be a Manager thereof (*i*).

## Chairman

10. (i) The Managers shall, at their first meeting in each year, elect two of their number to be respectively Chairman and Vice-Chairman of their meetings for the year. If the Chairman and Vice-Chairman are absent from any meeting, the members present shall, before any other business is transacted, choose one of their number to preside at that meeting. The Chairman and Vice-Chairman shall always be eligible for reappointment.

(ii) In the event of a casual vacancy in the office of Chairman or Vice-Chairman, the Managers shall, as soon as possible, elect a new Chairman or Vice-Chairman to hold office for the unexpired term of office of the Chairman or Vice-Chairman in whose place he is elected.

### Record of Managers present at Meetings

11. The names of the Managers present at a meeting of the Managers shall be recorded in the minutes of that meeting.

### Minutes of Meetings

12. The minutes of the proceedings of the Managers shall be open to inspection by the Local Education Authority (*j*) and the Managers shall, if requested by the Chief Education Officer so to do, forward a copy of the minutes to the Local Education Authority for their inspection.

### Rescinding Resolutions

13. Any resolution of the Managers may be rescinded or varied at a subsequent meeting if due notice of the intention to rescind or vary the same has been given to all the managers: Provided that if the resolution proposed to be rescinded or varied was passed during the previous six months, the notice shall be signed by at least a majority of the Managers.

### Adjournment of Meetings

14. If at the time appointed for a meeting a sufficient number of Managers to form a quorum is not present, or if at any meeting the business is not completed, the meeting shall stand adjourned *sine die*, and a special meeting shall be summoned as soon as conveniently may be. Any meeting may be adjourned by resolution.

### Meetings of Managers

15. The Managers shall, in addition to holding a meeting at least once in every school term as required by the provisions of the Fourth Schedule to the Act, hold such other meetings as may be necessary for the efficient discharge of their functions.

### Convening of Meetings

16. (i) Seven clear days (*k*) at least before a meeting of the Managers, a summons to attend the meeting, specifying the business proposed to be transacted thereat, and signed by the Correspondent to the Managers, shall be left at, or sent by post to, the usual place of residence of each Manager: Provided that in the case of a meeting of the Managers convened by any two of their number, in accordance with the provisions of the Fourth Schedule to the Act, the aforesaid summons shall be signed by the two Managers convening the meeting: Provided also that want of service of the summons on any Manager shall not affect the validity of a meeting.

(ii) At the same time as the aforesaid summons is dispatched, a copy of the Agenda shall be sent to the Chief Education Officer for his information.

### Revocation of Final Order (*l*)

17. The Final Order specified in the Schedule to this Instrument, so far as it relates to the school, is hereby revoked.

### Date of Instrument

18. The date of this Instrument shall be the date upon which it is established by an Order of the Secretary of State.

NOTE. – Meetings and proceedings of Managers are regulated by the provisions of the Fourth Schedule to the Act, as amended by the Education (Miscellaneous Provisions) Act, 1948, which are as follows:

'(1) The quorum of the managers or governors shall not be less than three, or one-third of the whole number of managers or governors, whichever is the greater.

(2) The proceedings of the managers or governors shall not be invalidated by any vacancy in their number or by any defect in the election, appointment or qualification of any manager or governor.

(3) Every question to be determined at a meeting of the managers or governors shall be determined by a majority of the votes of the managers or governors present and voting on the question, and where there is an equal division of votes the chairman of the meeting shall have a second or casting vote.

(4) The managers or governors shall hold a meeting at least once in every school term.

(5) A meeting of the managers or governors may be convened by any two of their number.

(6) The minutes of the proceedings of the managers or governors shall be kept in a book provided for that purpose.'

### Illustrations of the different constitutions of managing and governing bodies according to the classification and character of the schools

#### (1) Controlled Church of England Primary School

TWO Foundation Managers being:

One *ex-officio* Foundation Manager, being the Principal Officiating Minister of the ecclesiastical parish or district within which the school is for the time being situated: Provided that if the said Minister refuses to act, or is absent from all the meetings of the Managers during a period of twelve months, or there is a vacancy of the benefice, the Archdeacon of the Archdeaconry within which the school is situated may from time to time appoint some person to act as substitute for the said Minister for such period as he thinks fit; and

One person, being a member of the Church of England, to be appointed by the Y. Diocesan Education Committee after consultation with the Parochial Church Council of the said ecclesiastical parish or district; and

FOUR Representative Managers to be appointed:

Two by the Z. Parish Council (*m*), and

Two by the local education authority.

Managers, other than *ex-officio* Managers, need not be members of the appointing body.

#### (2) Controlled Methodist Primary School

TWO Foundation Managers being:

One *ex-officio* Manager, being the Superintendent Methodist Minister of the local Methodist Circuit or a Methodist Minister to be nominated in writing under his hand for a period not exceeding three years; and One Foundation Manager to be appointed by the trustees in whom the legal estate in the school premises is for the time being vested; and

FOUR Representative Managers to be appointed:

Two by the Z. Parish Council (*m*), and

Two by the local education authority.

Managers, other than *ex-officio* Managers, need not be members of the appointing body.

### (3) Controlled Undenominational Primary School

TWO Foundation Managers to be appointed by the Trustees in whom the legal estate in the school premises is for the time being vested; and

FOUR Representative Managers to be appointed:
Two by the Z. Parish Council (*m*), and
Two by the local education authority.

Managers need not be members of the appointing body.

### (4) Aided Church of England Primary School

FOUR Foundation Managers being:

One *ex-officio* Foundation Manager, being the Principal Officiating Minister of the ecclesiastical parish or district within which the school is for the time being situated: Provided that if the said Minister refuses to act, or is absent from all the meetings of the Managers during a period of twelve months, or there is a vacancy of the benefice, the Archdeacon of the Archdeaconry within which the School is situated may from time to time appoint some person to act as substitute for the said Minister for such period as he thinks fit; and

Three persons, being members of the Church of England, of whom two shall be appointed by the Y. Diocesan Education Committee, and one by the Parochial Church Council of the said ecclesiastical parish or district, and

TWO Representative Managers to be appointed:
One by the Z. Parish Council (*m*), and
One by the local education authority.

Managers, other than *ex-officio* Managers, need not be members of the respective appointing bodies.

### (5) Aided Roman Catholic Primary School

FOUR Foundation Managers to be appointed by the Trustees of the Roman Catholic Diocese of Y.; and

TWO Representative Managers to be appointed:
One by the Z. Parish Council (*m*), and
One by the local education authority.

A Manager need not be a member of the body by which he was appointed (*n*).

### (6) Controlled Secondary School (*o*)

TEN Representative Governors to be appointed by the local education authority (who may, if they see fit, appoint the Chairman of the Secondary Education Sub-Committee to be an *ex-officio* Governor) of whom:
One shall be appointed on the nomination of the A. Borough Council (*p*);
One shall be appointed on the nomination of the B. Urban District Council; and
One shall be appointed on the nomination of the C. Rural District Council; and

FIVE Foundation Governors to be appointed as follows:
One by the Council of the University of D.;
One by the Dean and Chapter of the Cathedral Church of E.;
One by the Methodist Education Committee; and
Two, except in the case of the undermentioned persons, who shall be deemed to be two of the first Foundation Governors, by the Foundation Governors for the time being in office.

The following persons shall be two of the first Foundation Governors and shall be entitled to hold office, subject to the provisions of this Instrument as to determination of governorship, for the periods, commencing at the date of this Instrument, respectively set against their names:

| | | | |
|---|---|---|---|
| F. G. of H. | .. | .. | 5 years |
| I. J. of K. | .. | .. | 4 years |

A Governor need not be a member of the appointing or nominating body.

### NOTES

(a) **County Council of the Administrative County**, or County Borough Council, or, in the Greater London area, the Council of the outer London Borough, or the Greater London Council, acting by means of a Special Committee.

(b) **Other than an *ex-officio* manager**, if the instrument provides for such an appointment.

(c) **Each for a term of three years**. – A longer term, say five years, may be appropriate in the case of foundation governors of secondary schools, but a shorter term than three years is not generally desirable.

(d) **Notified to the correspondent to the existing body of managers**, *i.e.* in the case of an existing school receiving its first instrument of management under the Education Act, 1944. In the case of a newly-established school, the name of the person, *e.g.* the Vicar of the Parish in the case of a Church of England school, is inserted as the person to whom the notification of appointments of the managers is to be sent.

(e) **Summoned by the said correspondent**, *i.e.* in the case of an existing school. In the case of a newly-established school, a named person, *e.g.* the Vicar of the Parish in the case of a Church of England school, is stated as the person to convene the first meeting.

(f) **Except in special circumstances**. – There is nothing to prevent any eligible person from becoming a manager or governor, but a manager or governor will be debarred from supplying work or goods to or for the school.

(g) **Remuneration for his services**. – A manager or governor may act as honorary correspondent or clerk, but if the correspondent or clerk is remunerated by the L.E.A. he may not be a manager or governor of the school. Official postages, stationery, and telephone calls of the correspondent or clerk, whether honorary or not, in connection with the maintenance of the school, are payable by the L.E.A. See S.114 (2) (a).

(h) **Other than an *ex-officio* manager**. – See note (b) above.

(i) **A manager thereof**, though not of some other school.

(j) **Open to inspection by the local education authority**. – As laid down by S.21 (3).

(k) **Seven clear days**, or other interval appropriate to the case.

(l) **Revocation of final order**. – In the case of an existing school for which such a 'final order' was made under an earlier Act. This is applicable to voluntary primary schools. In the case of a voluntary grammar school, the articles of government will contain a provision modifying the scheme made by the Board of Education under the Charitable Trusts Acts.

(m) **Parish council**, or other minor authority or authorities (see Chapter II, §2, note (e)). In the case of a county borough, all the representative managers are appointed by the L.E.A.

(n) **Need not be a member of the body by which he was appointed**. – But, in the case of Roman Catholic aided primary and secondary schools, and special agreement schools, the instrument also includes the provision that any foundation manager or governor who, in the opinion of the Roman Catholic ordinary of the Diocese wherein the school is situate, has ceased for the purposes of this clause (determination of managership or governorship) to be a member of the Roman Catholic Church, shall thereupon cease to be a manager or governor.

(o) **Controlled secondary school**. – Allowing for the statutory interchange of the majority as between representative and foundation governors, in the case of aided and special agreement schools, as compared with controlled schools, the provision to be made for the former schools is of the same general character as in this illustration. Representation of religious bodies and of a university will depend on the character of the original scheme, and the representations made by the L.E.A. and governors.

In the case of voluntary grammar schools, the modification made by the articles of government to the scheme made by the Board of Education under the Charitable

Trusts Acts will repeal most of the provisions of the scheme, as they are inconsistent with the Education Act, 1944. The constitution of the governing body under the old scheme for the purposes of the administration of the endowments will not be varied by the modifications made by the Secretary of State in the articles and, at least at first, there will be two governing bodies, one for the general government of the school under the Education Acts, the other for the administration of the endowments. In most cases it will be possible to arrange for common membership of both bodies for many of the governors; and, in due course, it may be that the Secretary of State with the assent of the governors acting under the old scheme will be able to arrange, in many cases, for the elimination of this division of functions.

(*p*) **Borough council.** – Representation of borough, urban and rural district councils will usually only be appropriate where the L.E.A. are a county council.

## II. *Specimen Rules of Management for a Controlled Primary School*

### Interpretations

1. In these Rules, unless the context otherwise requires, the following expressions shall have the meanings hereby assigned to them:

'The Act' means the Education Act, 1944, as amended by any subsequent enactment;

'The Local Education Authority' means the County Council of the Administrative County (*a*) of X., and, where a function has been delegated to a Committee of the County Council or to any Sub-Committee of such a Committee, includes in relation to such function the Committee or the Sub-Committee to whom the exercise of such function is delegated;

'Secretary of State' means the Secretary of State for Education and Science.

Other expressions to which meanings are assigned by the Act shall have the same meanings as are assigned to them in the Act.

The interpretation Act, 1889, shall apply to the interpretation of these Rules as it applies to an Act of Parliament.

### Conduct of School

2. The A.B. Primary School (hereinafter called 'the School') shall be maintained in or near the Parish of Z. and shall be conducted in accordance with: (i) the Act; (ii) the *Schools Regulations* for the time being in force and made by the Secretary of State under the Local Government Act, 1966; (iii) these Rules; (iv) any relevant provisions of the Trust Deed, if any, of the School, so far as such provisions are consistent with the Act and the aforesaid Regulations and these Rules; and (v) any regulations and directions of the local education authority made or given under the Act with respect to any matters not specifically provided for in these Rules.

### School Premises

3. The Managers shall from time to time inspect and keep the local education authority informed as to the condition and state of repair of the school premises, and, subject to the regulations of the local education authority, shall have power to carry out urgent repairs (*b*) up to such amount as may be approved by the local education authority.

### Appointment and Dismissal of Head Teacher

4. The appointment and dismissal of the Head Teacher shall conform to the following procedure:

(1) The local education authority shall, subject as hereinafter provided, advertise the vacant post and draw up a short list from the applications

received. The appointment of the Head Teacher shall be made by the local education authority, on the recommendation of a Joint Committee (*c*), consisting of the Primary Education Sub-Committee of the Education Committee of the local education authority and the Managers under the chairmanship of a person nominated by the local education authority: Provided that the local education authority may fill the vacancy by transferring a teacher from another school maintained by them after informing the Managers as to the person whom they propose to appoint and after considering any representations made by the Managers with respect to the proposed appointment.

(2) The Head Teacher shall be employed under a contract of service in writing (*d*) with the local education authority, determinable only (except in the case of dismissal for misconduct or any other urgent cause) upon three months' notice in writing by either side taking effect at the end of a Spring or Autumn term or upon four months' notice in writing by either side taking effect at the end of a Summer Term: Provided always that the local education authority may suspend the Head Teacher from his office for misconduct or any other urgent cause pending their decision on the question of the determination of his contract.

(3) The Head Teacher shall be entitled to appear, accompanied by a friend, at any meeting of the appropriate Sub-Committee of the Education Committee of the local education authority to which the question of his dismissal is referred. The Head Teacher shall be given at least seven clear days' notice of any such meeting.

### Assistant Masters

5. The appointment and dismissal of Assistant Masters (which expression shall for the purposes of these Rules include Assistant Mistresses) shall conform to the following procedure:

(1) The appointment of Assistant Masters shall be made by the local education authority: Provided that unless the Foundation Managers are satisfied as to the fitness and competence of any Assistant Master to give such religious instruction as is required to be given by a reserved teacher in the school the local education authority shall not appoint that person to be a reserved teacher in the school.

(2) Every Assistant Master shall be employed under a contract of service in writing (*d*) with the local education authority, determinable only (except in the case of dismissal for misconduct or any other urgent cause) upon two months' notice in writing by either side taking effect at the end of a Spring or Autumn term or upon three months' notice in writing by either side taking effect at the end of a Summer term.

(3) The procedure in connection with the termination of the employment, or the suspension, of Assistant Masters shall be the same as that hereinbefore specified for the Head Teacher.

(4) If the Foundation Managers are of opinion that any reserved teacher has failed to give such religious instruction as is required to be given by such a teacher in the school, efficiently and suitably, they may require the local education authority to determine his employment as a reserved teacher in the school.

### Correspondent

6. The local education authority shall appoint the Correspondent to the Managers on the recommendation of the Managers. The conditions of service and the

appointment of the Correspondent of the Managers shall be determinable by the local education authority, but the Managers shall be entitled to recommend his dismissal.

## Non-teaching Staff

7. The non-teaching staff of the School shall be appointed and dismissed by the local education authority on the recommendation of the Managers (e).

## Organization and Curriculum

8. (1) The local education authority shall, after consultation with the Managers, determine the educational character of the school, as a controlled school, and its place in the local education system, and subject thereto and to the provisions of these Rules and of the regulations and directions of the local education authority the Managers shall, in consultation with the Head Teacher, have the general direction of the conduct of the school. The Managers shall forthwith notify the local education authority of any matter in relation to the school in respect of which the Managers have not power to take the necessary action.

(2) Subject to the provisions of these Rules and of the regulations and directions of the local education authority, the Head Teacher shall control the internal organization, management and discipline of the school, shall exercise supervision over the teaching and non-teaching staff employed at the school, and shall have the power of suspending pupils from attendance for any cause which he considers adequate, but on suspending any pupil he shall forthwith report the case to the Managers, who shall notify the local education authority.

(3) (a) There shall be full consultation at all times between the Head Teacher and the Chairman of the Managers.

(b) All proposals and reports affecting the conduct of the school shall be submitted to the Managers. The Chief Education Officer shall be informed of such reports and proposals and be furnished with a copy thereof at least fourteen days before they are considered.

(c) The Head Teacher shall be entitled to attend throughout every meeting of the Managers, except on such occasions and for such times as the Managers may for good cause otherwise determine.

(d) Suitable arrangements shall be made for enabling the teaching staff to submit their views or proposals to the Managers through the Head Teacher.

## School Holidays

9. Holidays for the school shall be fixed by the local education authority, but the Managers shall have power to grant mid-term or other occasional holidays not exceeding the number of days specified by the local education authority in any year.

## Admission of Pupils

10. The Managers shall be responsible for the admission of pupils, so, however, that they shall act in accordance with arrangements agreed (f) with the local education authority.

## Returns

11. The Managers shall furnish to the local education authority such returns and reports as the local education authority may require.

## Copies of Rules

12. A copy of these Rules shall be given to every Manager, Head Teacher, and every Assistant Teacher on entry into office.

## Date of Rules

13. The date of the Rules shall be the date upon which they are established by an Order of the local education authority.

### NOTES

(a) **County council of the administrative county.** – See note (a) of Specimen Instrument of Management.

(b) **Urgent repairs.** – In a county borough it may be more convenient for the L.E.A. not to delegate this power.

(c) **On the recommendation of a joint committee.** – This procedure goes beyond the minimum requirement of the Act, which only requires that the L.E.A. shall inform the managers as to the person whom they propose to appoint and shall consider any representations made by the managers with respect to the proposed appointment. The procedure set out in this rule, however, provides not only for expeditious consultation, but allows the managers to attend and vote at the meeting of the interviewing sub-committee. The constitution of the joint committee may be arranged by the L.E.A. so as to give them a clear majority at least.

(d) **Contract of service in writing,** or minute if preferred.

(e) **Non-teaching staff.** – The L.E.A. may retain the direct power of appointment and dismissal of any of the non-teaching staff if they desire to do so.

(f) **Admission of pupils.** – The managers and L.E.A. must have regard to S.76, to the *Schools Regulations, 1959,* and to the *Pupils' Registration Regulations, 1948.*

# III. *Specimen Rules of Management for an Aided Primary School (a)*

### Interpretations

1. As Rule 1 of Controlled Primary School.

### Conduct of School

2. (1) The A.B. Primary School (hereinafter called 'the School') shall be maintained in or near the Parish of Z. and shall be conducted in accordance with: (i) the Act; (ii) the *Schools Regulations* for the time being in force and made by the Secretary of State under the Local Government Act, 1966; (iii) these Rules; (iv) any relevant provisions of the Trust Deed, if any, of the School, so far as such provisions are consistent with the Act and the aforesaid Regulations and these Rules; and (v) any regulations and directions of the local education authority made or given under the Act with respect to any matters not specifically provided for in these Rules.

(2) The religious observance and instruction in the School shall (subject to the provisions of the Act) be in accordance with the practices, rites and doctrines of the Y. Church.

### School Premises

1. (1) The Managers shall from time to time inspect and keep the local education authority informed as to the condition and state of repair of the school premises.

(2) With respect to repairs to, and alterations of, the school premises for which the local education authority are responsible under the Act:

   (i) the Managers shall have power, subject to the regulations of the local education authority, to carry out urgent repairs (b) up to such amount as may be approved by the local education authority;

   (ii) all alterations and all repairs not carried out under the provisions of the preceding sub-paragraph, shall be carried out by the local education authority.

## Appointment and Dismissal of Head Teacher

4. The appointment and dismissal of the Head Teacher shall conform to the following procedure:

(1) On the occurrence of a vacancy the Managers shall advertise the post, and shall draw up a short list from the applications received and shall interview the candidates on that list: Provided that the Managers shall invite the Chief Education Officer of the local education authority or his representative to attend the meeting at which the appointment of the Head Teacher is to be made to advise on the educational qualifications of the candidates on the short list, unless other arrangements have been agreed between the Managers and the local education authority for obtaining such advice.

(2) The Head Teacher shall, unless the Managers are of opinion that the post should be re-advertised, be appointed from the candidates on the short list: Provided that the local education authority may prohibit the appointment if they are not satisfied with his educational qualifications *(c)*.

(3) The Head Teacher shall be employed under a contract of service in writing with the Managers, which shall, except in the case of dismissal for misconduct or any other urgent cause, be determinable only upon three months' notice in writing by either side taking effect at the end of a Spring or Autumn Term, or upon four months' notice in writing by either side taking effect at the end of a Summer Term: Provided that the Managers may, by resolution, suspend the Head Teacher from his office for misconduct or any other urgent cause pending their decision on the question of the determination of his contract: Provided also that the local education authority shall have power to prohibit the dismissal of the Head Teacher without the consent of the local education authority and to require the dismissal of the Head Teacher.

(4) The Head Teacher shall be entitled to appear, accompanied by a friend, at any meeting of the Managers held to consider the termination of his employment, and at any meeting of the appropriate sub-committee of the Education Committee of the local education authority to which the question of his dismissal is referred *(d)*. The Head Teacher shall be given at least seven clear days' notice of any such meeting.

## Assistant Masters

5. The appointment and dismissal of Assistant Masters (which expression shall for the purposes of these Rules include Assistant Mistresses) shall conform to the following procedure:

(1) On the occurrence of a vacancy for an Assistant Master the post shall, except as hereinafter provided, be advertised and the appointment be made by the Managers to their service: Provided that the appointment may be made without advertisement if the Managers, with the consent of the local education authority, fill the post by appointing a teacher to their service from another school maintained by the local education authority or from any group of new entrants to the teaching profession selected by the local education authority: Provided also that the local education authority shall determine the limits of the establishment of staff *(e)* to be employed in the school, and may prohibit the appointment, without the consent of the local education authority, of any Assistant Master to be employed for giving secular instruction in the school *(f)*.

(2) Every Assistant Master shall be employed under a contract of service in writing with the Managers, which shall, except in the case of dismissal for misconduct or any other urgent cause, be determinable only upon two

months' written notice by either side taking effect at the end of a Spring or Autumn Term, or upon three months' written notice by either side taking effect at the end of a Summer Term: Provided that the Managers may, by resolution, suspend any Assistant Master from his office for misconduct or any other urgent cause pending their decision on the question of the determination of his contract: Provided also that the local education authority shall have power to require the dismissal of any Assistant Master and, except as otherwise provided in S.28 (2) of the Act (*g*), to prohibit the dismissal of an Assistant Master without the consent of the local education authority.

(3) The procedure in connection with the termination of the employment of Assistant Master shall be the same as that hereinbefore specified for the Head Teacher (*h*).

### Correspondent

6. The Correspondent to the Managers shall be appointed and dismissed by the Managers, subject to any directions that may be given by the local education authority with respect to his conditions of service relative to the maintenance of the school (*i*).

### Non-teaching Staff

7. The non-teaching staff of the school shall be appointed and dismissed by the Managers, subject to any directions which may be given by the local education authority with regard to the number and conditions of service of such staff (*j*).

### Organization and Curriculum

8. (1) The local education authority shall, in agreement with the Managers, determine the general educational character of the school, as an aided school, and its place in the local educational system. Subject thereto, and to the provisions of these Rules and of the regulations and directions made or given by the local education authority under the Act (*k*), the Managers shall, in consultation with the Head Teacher, have the general direction of the conduct and curriculum of the school. The Managers shall forthwith notify the local education authority of any matter in relation to the school in respect of which the Managers have not power to take any necessary action.

(2) Subject to the provisions of these Rules and of the regulations and directions made or given by the local education authority under the Act (*k*), the Head Teacher shall control the internal organization, management, and discipline of the school, shall exercise supervision over the teaching and non-teaching staff employed at the school, and shall have the power of suspending pupils from attendance for any cause which he considers adequate, but on suspending any pupil he shall forthwith report the case to the Managers, who shall thereupon notify the local education authority.

(3) (*a*) There shall be full consultation at all times between the Head Teacher and the Chairman of the Managers.

(*b*) All proposals and reports affecting the conduct of the school shall be submitted to the Managers. The Chief Education Officer shall be informed of such reports and proposals and be furnished with a copy thereof at least fourteen days before they are considered.

(*c*) The Head Teacher shall be entitled to attend throughout every meeting of the Managers, except on such occasions and for such times as the Managers may for good cause otherwise determine.

(*d*) Suitable arrangements shall be made for enabling the teaching staff to submit their views or proposals to the Managers through the Head Teacher.

### School Holidays

9. Holidays for the school shall be fixed by the local education authority (*l*), but the Managers shall have power to grant mid-term or other occasional holidays not exceeding the number of days specified by the local education authority in any year.

### Admission of Pupils

10. The Managers shall be responsible for the admission of pupils, so, however, that they shall act in accordance with arrangements agreed (*m*) with the local education authority.

### Returns

11. As Rule 11 of Controlled Primary School.

### Copies of Rules

12. As Rule 12 of Controlled Primary School.

### Date of Rules

13. As Rule 13 of Controlled Primary School.

### NOTES

(*a*) **Rules of management for an aided school.** – The rules are made by the L.E.A. without reference to the Secretary of State – see S.17 (1) (*b*) – and there are only two matters on which the L.E.A. are required to consult the managers before making the rules, *viz.* – see S.24 (2) (*b*) – the rule concerning the power of the L.E.A. to prohibit the appointment, without the consent of the L.E.A., of teachers to be employed for giving secular instruction; and the rule enabling the L.E.A. to give directions as to the educational qualifications of the teachers to be so employed.

Apart from that, the L.E.A. are entitled to make the rules of management without reference to any other body, but the rules made must not, of course, conflict with the provisions of the Act, or with the Regulations of the Secretary of State.

We have not included in these specimen rules, any rule relating to equipment etc. It is open to the L.E.A. to include such a rule if desired. The regulations of the L.E.A. regarding books and materials must give the managers, in consultation with the head teacher, freedom of choice of books and materials, subject to the contracts of the L.E.A. for supplies. The L.E.A. may prefer to reserve to themselves the choice of furniture and other equipment for the school.

(*b*) **Repairs.** – In a county borough it may be more convenient not to delegate this power to the managers.

It may be noticed that it is the custom in making rules of management, to refer only to repairs and alterations for which the L.E.A. are responsible. But it should be noted that with regard to the external repairs for which the managers are responsible, it is expedient that the L.E.A. should exercise supervision over them, to ensure that they are carried out without delay, and, in regard to painting and decoration, no less frequently than in the case of a county school. Not only because it is wise to do so, or because an 80 per cent grant is now available from the Secretary of State to the managers towards the work, but because neglect to attend to external repairs may result in the need for internal repairs for which the L.E.A., not the managers, are responsible. There is no need nowadays to accept different standards of maintenance for county and voluntary schools.

(*c*) **Prohibit the appointment.** – The power to do so derives from S.24 (2) (*b*), after consultation with the managers in preparing the rules of management.

(*d*) **Question of his dismissal is referred.** – If the question of dismissal arises solely on the particular religious grounds specified in S.28 (2), it is a matter solely for the managers, but see Chapter II, §6, note (*m*). Otherwise it is also a matter for the L.E.A., and the L.E.A. can require the managers to dismiss.

(*e*) **Establishment of staff.** – The L.E.A. control by S.24 (2) (*a*).

(*f*) **Secular instruction in the school.** – The power of the L.E.A. derives from S.24 (2) (*b*).

(*g*) **Except as otherwise provided in S.28 (2) of the Act.** – See note (*d*) above.

(*h*) **Hereinbefore specified for the head teacher.** – See Rule 4 (4) above.

(*i*) **Relative to the maintenance of the school.** – If a manager is appointed as honorary correspondent, there is no question of remuneration. If a person, other than a manager, is appointed correspondent, his remuneration for his duties and expenses relative to the maintenance of the school is an obligation on the L.E.A. under S.114 (2) (*a*), and it is for the L.E.A. to define such duties and determine his remuneration.

(*j*) **Of such staff.** – If provision is made by the L.E.A. on the lines of this rule to delegate so much power to the managers the following points should be noted: (i) the caretaker and cleaners are appointed to the service of the managers, and they have the exclusive right of appointment and dismissal. The provisions of S.30, barring disqualification for appointment on religious grounds, apply to such appointments as to all other non-teaching staff; (ii) school meals staff must be appointed to the services of the L.E.A. by Regulation 13 of the *Provision of Milk and Meals Regulations, 1945,* (iii) as playing fields are the property of the L.E.A., groundsmen may be appointed to their service. If the L.E.A. are not prepared to delegate to the managers the powers set out in the rule given here they can limit the powers of managers to the appointment and dismissal of the caretaker and cleaners.

(*k*) **Regulations and directions made or given by the local education authority.** – The regulations and directions of the L.E.A. in this respect are not confined to the matter of secular instruction. They extend to all matters, under the Act, save those relating to the religious observance and instruction required to be observed and given in the school by virtue of its being an aided school.

(*l*) **Holidays shall be fixed by the local education authority.** – By virtue of S.23 (1) and S.23 (3). The holidays must be fixed in conformity with Regulation 11 of the *Schools Regulations, 1959,* made by the Secretary of State.

(*m*) **Arrangements agreed with the local education authority.** – Obviously the sooner arrangements are agreed, the better. But it must not be supposed that until agreement has been reached in any case, the managers may admit any child for whom there is a vacancy. If the journey involved for a child is unreasonable, it is unreasonable under the Act, before, as well as after, agreement under this rule has been reached between the L.E.A. and the managers. In towns, zoning may feature in the agreement, so as to define areas to be served by more than one aided school of the same denomination. Otherwise, under S.76 and the advice given by the Secretary of State on it in the *Manual of Guidance No. 1* on the Choice of Schools, a journey for a primary school child of more than three-quarters of an hour from leaving home to the beginning of the school session, and, similarly, for the return journey, is regarded as the maximum limit normally to be allowed under arrangements made under this rule.

# IV. *Specimen Articles of Government for a Controlled Secondary School*

## Interpretations

1. As Rule 1 for Controlled Primary School.

## Conduct of School

2. The A.B. Secondary School (hereinafter called 'the School') which shall be a day school for boys and girls, shall be maintained in or near the Urban District of Z. and shall be conducted in accordance with: (i) The Act; (ii) the *Schools Regulations* for the time being in force and made by the Secretary of State under the Local Government Act, 1966; and (iii) these Articles.

## Finance

3. (i) The Governors shall submit to the local education authority, at such times and in such form as may be required by the local education authority, estimates of the income and expenditure required for the purposes of the School.

(ii) The Governors shall, subject to any Regulations of the local education authority, be entitled to incur expenditure within the several limits of the amounts specified under each head of the estimates approved by the local education authority. The Governors shall not exeed the amount approved by the local education authority under any head of the estimates in any year without the previous consent of the local education authority.

(iii) The local education authority shall be responsible for the making of all payments and the keeping of all accounts in respect of the maintenance of the School and shall furnish to the Governors such periodic returns of payments made by the authority as will enable the Governors to comply with the provisions of paragraph (ii) of this Article.

(iv) Where under any Regulations of the local education authority the Governors are authorized to undertake the collection of moneys due to the local education authority, the Governors shall pay such moneys into the County Fund.

## School Premises

4. The Governors shall from time to time inspect and keep the local education authority informed as to the condition and state of repair of the school premises, and in such circumstances as may be specified in Regulations of the local education authority the Governors shall have power to carry out repairs (*a*) to the school premises.

## Appointment and Dismissal of Head Master

5. The appointment and dismissal of the Head Master shall conform to the following procedure:

(i) The vacant post shall be advertised by the local education authority and a short list shall be drawn up from the applications for the post by a Joint Committee (*b*) consisting of an equal number of Governors and representatives of the local education authority under the chairmanship of a person nominated by the local education authority. The said Joint Committee shall also meet to interview the persons on the short list and shall, unless they are of opinion that the post should be re-advertised, recommend one person on the list for appointment by the local education authority.

(ii) The Head Master shall be employed under a contract of service (*c*) in writing with the local education authority, which shall, subject to any provisions relating to retirement and except in the case of dismissal for misconduct or any other urgent cause, be determinable only upon three months' notice in writing by either side taking effect at the end of a Spring or Autumn Term or upon four months' notice in writing by either side taking effect at the end of a Summer term: Provided always that the Governors may at any time make a recommendation to the local education authority that the Head Master should be dismissed for misconduct or any other urgent cause or should be given notice as aforesaid, and may by resolution suspend the Head Master from his office for misconduct or any other urgent cause pending the decision of the local education authority. Provided also that the local education authority shall consult the Governors before any decision is taken to dismiss, or give notice to, the Head Master.

(iii) A resolution of the Governors to recommend the termination of the Head Master's employment shall not take effect until it has been confirmed at a meeting of the Governors held not less than fourteen days after the date of the meeting at which the resolution was passed.

(iv) Where a meeting of the Governors or of the local education authority is held to consider the termination of the Head Master's employment in such circumstances as may be specified in regulations of the local education authority, the Head Master shall, in accordance with such procedure as may be specified in the said regulations, be entitled to appear, accompanied by a friend, at any such meeting.

### Assistant Masters

6. The appointment and dismissal of Assistant Masters (which expression shall for the purposes of these Articles include Assistant Mistresses) shall conform to the following procedure (*d*):

(i) On the occurrence of a vacancy for an Assistant Master, the Governors shall notify the local education authority who shall, unless they are of opinion that the vacancy should not be filled, advertise the post, and shall transmit to the Governors the names of the candidates: Provided that the local education authority may, if they think fit, and after giving full consideration to the views of the Governors and the Head Master, and subject to S.27 (4) of the Act relating to reserved teachers, require the Governors to appoint a Master to be transferred from another school maintained by the local education authority or from any group of new entrants to the teaching profession selected by the local education authority.

(ii) The appointment of Assistant Masters shall be made to the service of the local education authority by the Governors in consultation with the Head Master, within the limits of the establishment of staff laid down from time to time by the local education authority, and such appointments shall, except where made under paragraph (i) of this Article, be subject to the approval of the local education authority.

(iii) Assistant Masters shall be employed under a contract of service (*e*) in writing with the local education authority, which shall, subject to any provisions relating to retirement, and except in the case of dismissal for misconduct or any other urgent cause, be determinable only upon two months' notice in writing by either side taking effect at the end of a Spring or Autumn Term or upon three months' notice in writing by either side taking effect at the end of a Summer Term.

(iv) The procedure in connection with the termination of the employment, or the suspension, of Assistant Masters shall be similar to that hereinbefore specified for the Head Master, except that two meetings of the Governors shall not be required.

(v) The appointment of any Assistant Master to be employed partly at the school and partly at another school maintained by the local education authority shall be made by the local education authority in consultation with the Governors of the schools concerned.

### Clerk to the Governors

7. The Clerk to the Governors (*f*) shall be appointed to the service of the local education authority by the Governors, after consultation with the local education authority, and shall be dismissed by the local education authority upon the recommendation of the Governors.

### Non-teaching Staff

8. The non-teaching staff of the School shall be appointed and dismissed by the local education authority after consultation with the Head Master and the Governors (*g*).

### Organization and Curriculum

9. (i) The local education authority, after consultation with the Governors, shall determine the general educational character of the School and its place in the

local educational system. Subject thereto, the Governors shall, in consultation with the Head Master, have the general direction of the conduct and curriculum of the School.

(ii) Subject to the provisions of these Articles, the Head Master shall control the internal organization, management and discipline of the School, shall exercise supervision over the teaching and non-teaching staff employed at the School, and shall have the power of suspending pupils from attendance for any cause which he considers adequate, but on suspending any pupil the parent shall be informed that he has a right of appeal to the Governors and a report of the case shall forthwith be made to the Governors, who shall thereupon consult the local education authority.

(iii) There shall be full consultation at all times between the Head Master and the Chairman of the Governors.

(iv) All proposals and reports affecting the conduct and curriculum of the School shall be submitted by the Head Master to the Governors. The Chief Education Officer shall be informed of such reports and proposals and be furnished with a copy thereof at least seven days before they are considered by the Governors.

(v) The Head Master shall be entitled to attend throughout every meeting of the Governors, except on such occasions and for such times as the Governors may for good cause otherwise determine.

(vi) There shall be full consultation and co-operation between the Head Master and the Chief Education Officer on matters affecting the welfare of the School.

(vii) Suitable arrangements shall be made for enabling the teaching staff to submit their views or proposals to the Governors through the Head Master.

### School Holidays

10. Holidays for the School (h) shall be fixed by the local education authority, but the Governors shall have power to grant mid-term or other occasional holidays not exceeding in any year the number of days approved by the local education authority.

### Admission of Pupils

11. The Governors shall be responsible for the admission of pupils so, however, that they shall act in accordance with arrangements agreed with the local education authority (i).

### Returns

12. The Governors shall furnish to the local education authority such returns and reports as the local education authority may require.

### Modification of Scheme

13. The Scheme specified in the Schedule hereto is hereby repealed to the extent specified therein (j).

### Copies of Articles

14. A copy of these Articles shall be given to every Governor, the Head Master and every Assistant Master on entry into office.

### Date of Articles

15. The date of these Articles shall be the date upon which they are established by an order of the Minister.

### NOTES

(a) **Power to carry out repairs.** – Alternatively, the articles may provide for the governors to carry out urgent repairs only up to such amount as may be approved by the L.E.A.; or, in the case of a county borough, it may be more convenient for the L.E.A. and governors to reserve the power to carry out repairs to the L.E.A. The articles of government are made by the Secretary of State under S.17 (3) (b), and the L.E.A. have the opportunity in this as in all other provisions of the articles to make suggestions on the draft articles to suit their local administration.

(b) **By a joint committee.** – This joint committee, or at least the joint committee by whom the short list is interviewed, may be so constituted as to provide that all the governors shall be members of it. For example, if there are fifteen governors, namely, five foundation governors and ten representative governors (of whom, say, six are members of the L.E.A.), a joint committee of eighteen persons, consisting of the five foundation governors, the four representative governors who are not members of the L.E.A., the six representative governors who are members of the L.E.A., and three other representatives of the L.E.A., would comply with the article and would give an interviewing committee of reasonable size. Alternatively, the article may provide for the governors (the majority of whom may be members of the L.E.A.) to make the short list, interview and recommend to the L.E.A. the person for appointment.

(c) **Contract of service,** or minute if preferred.

(d) **Shall conform to the following procedure.** – An alternative provision for paragraphs (i) and (ii) of this article, is as follows: '(i) On the occurrence of a vacancy for an assistant master the governors shall notify the local education authority who shall, unless they are of opinion that the vacancy should not be filled, advertise the post, the applications for which shall be received by the clerk to the governors; (ii) the appointment of assistant masters shall be made to the service of the local education authority by the governors in consultation with the head master within the limits of the establishment of staff laid down from time to time by the local education authority, and such appointments shall be subject to the approval of the local education authority.' This alternative arrangement precludes the L.E.A. from transferring a teacher from another school to the school in question, and from allocating a new recruit to the teaching profession, selected by the L.E.A., to the school, but it does not rule out the possibility of such a transfer or allocation with the agreement of the governors.

(e) **Contract of service,** or minute if preferred.

(f) **Clerk to the governors.** – The method of appointment of the clerk to the governors, and the provision therefor in the articles of government, will depend on local circumstances. In some cases the L.E.A. will wish to make the appointment themselves, and may wish to appoint their Chief Education Officer as clerk. In other cases, the L.E.A. may wish to leave the appointment entirely in the hands of the governors. The position of the clerk as regards any foundation work should be noted, and in modifying an old grammar school scheme, the Secretary of State will not, at this stage, repeal the provision relating to the clerk, with respect to foundation work. See also note (o) to Part I of this Appendix.

(g) **Other non-teaching staff.** – The L.E.A. may prefer that these powers shall be delegated to the governors, or, at least, as regards some of the non-teaching staff. Much depends, for example, on the method of organizing the school meals service of the L.E.A. Whatever the form of the article, the staff are to be appointed to the service of the L.E.A., and their number and conditions of service are determined by the L.E.A.

(h) **Holidays for the school.** – See note (l) to Part III of this Appendix.

(i) **Admission of pupils.** – The arrangements must take account of S.76, the *Schools Regulations, 1959*, and the *Pupils' Registration Regulations, 1948*.

(j) **Modification of scheme.** – In the case of secondary schools, which, previous to the Education Act, 1944, were conducted under a scheme made by the Board of Education, a Schedule to the Articles will specify which provisions of the old scheme are repealed.

# V. *Specimen Articles of Government for an Aided Secondary School*

## Interpretations

1. As Rule 1 for Controlled Primary School.

## Conduct of School

2. (1) The X. School, which shall be a day school for boys and girls, shall be maintained in or near the Y. Parish. The School shall be conducted in accordance

with (i) the Act; (ii) the *Schools Regulations* for the time being in force and made by the Secretary of State under the Local Government Act, 1966; (iii) these Articles; and (iv) any relevant provisions of the Trust Deed, if any, of the School, so far as such provisions are consistent with the Act and the aforesaid Regulations and these Articles.

(2) The religious observance and instruction in the School shall (subject to the provisions of the Act) be in accordance with the practices, rites, and doctrines of the Z. Church.

## Finance

3. (i) The Governors shall submit to the local education authority, at such times and in such form as may be required by the local education authority, estimates of the income and expenditure required for the purposes of the School.

(ii) With respect to expenditure to be borne by the local education authority (*a*) the Governors shall, subject to any Regulations of the local education authority, be entitled to incur expenditure within the several limits of the amounts specified under each head of the estimates as approved by the local education authority, and with respect to such expenditure, the Governors shall not exceed the amount approved by the local education authority under any head of the said estimates in any year without the previous consent of the local education authority.

(iii) The local education authority shall be responsible for the making of all payments and the keeping of all accounts in respect of the maintenance of the School, other than payments and accounts relating to expenditure for which the Governors are responsible under S.15 (3) (*a*) of the Act, and the local education authority shall furnish to the Governors such periodic returns of payments made by the authority as will enable the Governors to comply with the provisions of paragraph (ii) of this Article.

(iv) Where the Governors undertake the collection of moneys due to the local education authority, they shall pay such moneys to the local education authority.

## Equipment etc.

4. The Governors shall, in consultation with the Head Master, be responsible for the choice of books, stationery, furniture, apparatus, and other school materials, and where any particular articles of the categories aforesaid which the Governors require can conveniently and economically be obtained under the purchasing arrangements made by the local education authority, then the Governors shall obtain such article accordingly.

## School Premises

5. (i) The Governors shall from time to time inspect, and keep the local education authority informed as to the condition and state of repair of the school premises.

(ii) With respect to repairs to, and alterations of, the school premises for which the local education authority are responsible under the Act:

    (*a*) where the cost of the work does not exceed such an amount as may be decided from time to time by the local education authority, the Governors shall have power to execute the work; and

    (*b*) where the cost of the work exceeds the amount aforesaid, the work shall be carried out by the local education authority.

## Appointment and Dismissal of Head Master

6. The appointment and dismissal of the Head Master shall conform to the following procedure:

    (i) On the occurrence of a vacancy the Governors shall advertise the post, and shall draw up a short list from the applications received and shall interview the applicants on that list: Provided that the Governors shall invite the Chief Education Officer or his representative to attend the meeting at which the appointment of the Head Master is to be made to advise on the educational qualifications of the candidates on the short list, unless other arrangements have been agreed between the Governors and the local education authority for obtaining such advice.

(ii) The Head Master shall, unless the Governors are of the opinion that the post should be re-advertised, be appointed by the Governors from the candidates on the short list: Provided that the local education authority may prohibit the appointment if they are not satisfied with his educational qualifications (b).

(iii) The Head Master shall be employed under a contract of service in writing with the Governors which shall, except in the case of dismissal for misconduct or any other urgent cause, be determinable only upon three months' notice in writing by either side taking effect at the end of a Spring or Autumn term or upon four months' notice in writing by either side taking effect at the end of a Summer Term: Provided that the local education authority shall have power to prohibit the dismissal of the Head Master without the consent of the local education authority and to require the dismissal of the Head Master (c).

(iv) A resolution of the Governors to terminate the Head Master's employment shall not take effect until it has been confirmed at a meeting of the Governors held not less than fourteen days after the date of the meeting at which the resolution was passed. The Governors may, by resolution, suspend the Head Master from his office for misconduct or any other urgent cause pending the decision of the Governors on the question of the termination of his employment as aforesaid.

(v) The Head Master shall be entitled to appear, accompanied by a friend, at any meeting of the Governors held to consider the termination of his employment, and shall be entitled to appear, accompanied by a friend, at any meeting of the appropriate Sub-Committee of the Education Committee of the local education authority to which the question of his dismissal is referred. The Head Master shall be given at least seven clear days' notice of any such meetings.

### Assistant Masters

7. The appointment and dismissal of Assistant Masters (which expression shall for the purposes of these Articles include Assistant Mistresses) shall conform to the following procedure:

(i) On the occurrence of a vacancy for an Assistant Master, the Governors shall, if they think fit, advertise the post. The appointment, whether from the applications so received or otherwise, shall be made by the Governors to their service after consultation with the Head Master: Provided that the local education authority shall determine the limits of the establishment of staff to be employed in the school and may give directions to the Governors as to the educational qualifications of the staff (d).

(ii) Assistant Masters shall be employed under a contract of service in writing with the Governors. Appointments of Assistant Masters shall, except in the case of dismissal for misconduct or any other urgent cause, be determinable only upon two months' notice in writing by either side taking effect at the end of a Spring or Autumn term or upon three months' notice in writing by either side taking effect at the end of a Summer term: Provided that the local education authority shall have power to require the dismissal of any Assistant Master and, except as otherwise provided in S.28 (2) of the Act, to prohibit the dismissal of an Assistant Master without the consent of the local education authority (*e*).

(iii) The procedure in connection with the termination of the employment, or the suspension, of Assistant Masters shall be the same as that hereinbefore specified for the Head Master, except that two meetings of the Governors shall not be required.

### Non-teaching Staff

8. (i) The non-teaching staff of the school shall be appointed and dismissed by the Governors, subject to any directions which may be given by the local education authority with regard to the number and conditions of service of such staff (*f*).

(ii) The Clerk to the Governors shall be appointed and dismissed by the Governors, so, however, that his remuneration in respect of his duties in relation to the maintenance of the school shall be determined by the local education authority.

### Organization and Curriculum

9. (i) Subject to the provisions of the Development Plan approved for the area by the Minister as to the educational character of the school as an aided school and its place in the local educational system, the Governors shall, in consultation with the Head Master, have the general direction of the conduct and curriculum of the school.

(ii) Subject to the provisions of these Articles, the Head Master shall control the internal organization, management and discipline of the school, shall exercise supervision over the teaching and non-teaching staff, other than the Clerk to the Governors, and shall have the power of suspending pupils from attendance for any cause which he considers adequate, but on the suspension of any pupil the parent shall be informed that he has a right of appeal to the Governors, and a report of the case shall forthwith be made to the Governors, who shall thereupon consult the local education authority.

(iii) There shall be full consultation at all times between the Head Master and the Chairman of the Governors.

(iv) All proposals and reports affecting the conduct and curriculum of the school shall be submitted by the Head Master to the Governors, and any such proposals and reports involving questions of substance shall be submitted to the local education authority by the Governors, who shall consider any representations made by the local education authority before reaching a decision.

(v) The Head Master shall be entitled to attend throughout every meeting of the Governors, except on such occasions and for such times as the Governors may for good cause otherwise determine.

(vi) Suitable arrangements shall be made for enabling the teaching staff to submit their views or proposals to the Governors through the Head Master.

### School Holidays

10. The Governors shall have power to fix the holidays between terms and to grant such mid-term and other occasional holidays as they think fit (*g*), so, however, that the aggregate amount of holidays in any year shall be determined by the local education authority.

### Admission of Pupils

11. The Governors shall be responsible for the admission of pupils so, however, that they shall act in accordance with arrangements agreed with the local education authority (*h*), which shall, in particular, specify the circumstances in which, without the matter being specially referred to the local education authority,

pupils who belong to the area of some other local education authority may be admitted.

## Returns

12. As Article 12 for Controlled Secondary School.

## Modification of Scheme

13. As Article 13 for Controlled Secondary School.

## Copies of Articles

14. As Article 14 for Controlled Secondary School.

## Date of Articles

15. As Article 15 for Controlled Secondary School.

## NOTES

(*a*) **To be borne by the local education authority.** – The L.E.A. are responsible for the maintenance expenditure of the school, by S.114 (2) (*a*). But foundation income and expenditure of the governors is not subject to the control of the L.E.A. by S.65.

(*b*) **Directions as to his educational qualifications.** – This is included in the articles of government by agreement between the L.E.A. and the governors, under S.24 (2) (*b*), or, in default of such agreement, if the Secretary of State, who makes the articles, so determines.

(*c*) **Power of local education authority regarding the dismissal of the head master.** – See note (*d*) of Part III of this Appendix.

(*d*) **Directions as to their educational qualifications.** – See note (*b*) above, which applies also to assistant masters.

(*e*) **Without the consent of the local education authority.** – This is required by S.24 (2) (*a*), except where the dismissal is on the specific religious grounds set out in S.28 (2). See also Chapter II, §6, note (*m*).

(*f*) **Number and conditions of service of such staff.** – By S.22 (4) as regards caretakers and cleaners. As regards the school meals staff, the article may provide, if the school meals service arrangements of the L.E.A. so require, for the appointments to be made by the L.E.A. In any event the appointments of school meals staff are made to the service of the L.E.A. under the *Provision of Milk and Meals Regulations, 1945.*

(*g*) **Holidays.** – The provision that the aggregate amount of holidays shall be determined by the L.E.A. is made by the Secretary of State.

The holidays in aggregate allowed by the L.E.A. cannot normally exceed fourteen weeks in a year including mid-term and occasional holidays. See Regulation 11 of the *Schools Regulations, 1959.*

(*h*) **Admission of pupils.** – See note (*m*) of Part III of this Appendix. For a secondary school pupil, a journey of up to one and a quarter hours from leaving home to the beginning of the school session, and, similarly, for the return journey, is regarded by the Secretary of State as the maximum limit normally to be allowed under arrangements made under this article.

If the aided secondary school is a selective school, the arrangements will also make provision for the L.E.A. to be satisfied about the educational standards of pupils to be admitted.

# VI. *Specimen Articles of Government for a Special Agreement Secondary School*

## Interpretations

1. As Rule 1 for Controlled Primary School.

## Conduct of School

2. As Article 2 for Aided Secondary School.

### Finance

3. As Article 3 for Aided Secondary School.

### Equipment etc.

4. As Article 4 for Aided Secondary School.

### School Premises

5. As Article 5 for Aided Secondary School.

### Appointment and Dismissal of Head Master

6. As Article 5 for Controlled Secondary School (*a*).

### Assistant Masters

7. The appointment and dismissal of Assistant Masters (which expression shall for the purposes of these Articles include Assistant Mistresses) shall conform to the following procedure:

- (i) On the occurrence of a vacancy for an Assistant Master, the Governors shall notify the local education authority who shall, unless they are of opinion that the vacancy should not be filled, advertise the post, and shall transmit to the Governors the applications of the candidates: Provided that the local education authority may, if they think fit and after giving full consideration to the views of the Governors and the Head Master, and subject to S.28 (3) of the Act relating to reserved teachers (*b*), require the Governors to appoint a Master to be transferred from another school maintained by the local education authority or from any group of new entrants to the teaching profession selected by the local education authority.

- (ii) The appointment of Assistant Masters shall be made to the service of the local education authority by the Governors, in consultation with the Head Master, within the limits of the establishment of staff laid down from time to time by the local education authority, and such appointments shall, except where made under the proviso to paragraph (i) of this Article, be subject to the approval of the local education authority.

- (iii) Assistant Masters shall be employed under a contract of service in writing with the local education authority which shall, subject to any provisions relating to retirement, and except in the case of dismissal for misconduct or any other urgent cause, be determinable only upon two months' notice in writing by either side taking effect at the end of a Spring or Autumn Term, or upon three months' notice in writing by either side taking effect at the end of a Summer Term.

- (iv) The procedure in connection with the termination of the employment, or the suspension, of Assistant Masters shall be similar to that hereinbefore specified for the Head Master, except that two meetings of the Governors shall not be required.

- (v) The appointment of any Assistant Master to be employed partly at the School and partly at another school maintained by the local education authority shall be made by the local education authority in consultation with the Governors of the schools concerned.

### Clerk to the Governors

8. As Article 7 for Controlled Secondary School.

### Non-teaching Staff

9. As Article 8 for Controlled Secondary School.

## Organization and Curriculum

10. (i) Subject to the provisions of the Development Plan approved by the Secretary of State for the area in which the school is situate, and of any Local Education Order made by the Secretary of State for that area and for the time being in force specifying the general educational character of the school as a special agreement school, the Governors shall, in consultation with the Head Master, have the general direction of the conduct and curriculum of the School.

(ii) to (vii) As paragraphs (ii) to (vii) of Article 9 for Controlled Secondary School.

## Holidays

11. As Article 10 for Controlled Secondary School.

## Admission of Pupils

12. As Article 11 for Aided Secondary School.

## Returns

13. As Article 12 for Controlled Secondary School.

## Copies of Articles

14. As Article 13 for Controlled Secondary School.

## Date of Articles

15. As Article 14 for Controlled Secondary School.

## NOTES

(a) **Appointment and dismissal of head master.** – If the head master of a special agreement school is to be a reserved teacher, the agreement made under the Third Schedule to the Act – see §7 of the Schedule – will provide accordingly. In that case, S.28 (3) and S.28 (4) will apply with respect to the powers of the foundation governors relative to the appointment and dismissal of the head master on religious grounds.

(b) **Reserved teachers.** – As regards any reserved assistant masters (for whose appointment provision will be made in the agreement made under the Third Schedule to the Act), the powers of the foundation governors relative to their appointment and dismissal on religious grounds are the same as in the case of a reserved head master, under the same provisions of the Act. See note (a) above.